DOG TRAINING BIBLE

The Proven Path to a Happy and Obedient Dog - Discover the Secrets to Raise the Perfect Dog | Puppy Training, Mental Exercises, Dog Food, K9 Training, Positive Reinforcement

SANDY SCOTTISH

TABLE OF CONTENTS

Introduction

This is a complete practical guide about dog training. You can find here all you have to know about our amazing dogs and how to educate them at the best.

These complete dog training bibles, for letting you get all the tools, all the information and all the practices, will be divided into six very interesting books:

1. The first one will be all about puppy training: We will start right from the basics and that is when our beloved dogs are still small and can receive the correct education.
2. With the second guide, however, we will move on to the actual training as adults.
3. The third guide will cover a fundamental part that regards mental exercises for our dogs: in fact, we will see how dogs need both physical and mental exercise to stay healthy and happy.
4. The fourth guide will be entirely dedicated to dog food homestead.
5. The fifth will cover a topic truly important: dog healthy guidelines.
6. We will end this dog training bible with the real dog mental health.

In short, in this guide you will find every aspect concerning the health, nutrition, education and well-being of our dogs. If you want to be an attentive owner, who wants to take perfect care of your big puppy, look after his needs and make the most of this intelligent animal, you're in the right place! By the end of reading these six guides, you will be perfectly able to understand how to train and treat your beloved dog in the best possible way... Enjoy the reading!

PART 1: DOG TRAINING (PUPPY)

Introduction

We begin to take care of the well-being and education of our dog as a puppy. And this is precisely the purpose of this first guide: to make you understand the importance of training a puppy dog, the importance of having one and also understand what your responsibilities are. However, every aspect will be explained in detail to give you an idea of whether to get a puppy or not and how to train it.

Chapter 1: Introduction to Dog Ownership

This chapter provides an overview of the responsibilities of owning a dog, such as providing food, shelter, and medical care. It also covers selecting the right breed depending entirely on your lifestyle and home environment and preparing your home for a new dog.

Overview of the responsibilities of owning a dog

Owning a dog is one of the most beautiful sensations you can experience: a dog can offer all its love and affection and, if well trained, can give great satisfaction.

Loyal, faithful and obedient, the dog can be an excellent example of life for all family members and especially for the little ones. A lovely obedient, polite and helpful animal. It's the dog who, when he arrives at home, after an adoption, whether he's a puppy or an adult, begins to contribute to the well-being of family life and be an example of life just like a human.

But there are times when dogs surpass us and really succeed by character, temperament and innate qualities in teaching us humans how to live.

To quote some of the most famous phrases about owning a dog we have: "Anyone who hasn't had a dog doesn't know what it means to be loved". "A dog is all in his eyes." These are just some of the phrases that can theoretically explain this wonderful sensation: but to experience it yourself, you will have already owned dogs in the past, or you wish to have one dog now.

Whatever your case, know that dogs fill your life: with joy, affection and loyalty!

But we need to pay close attention to a truly vital basic concept: having a dog above all entails responsibilities. Because it's not just the beauty of having a wonderful, loving and above all very sweet purebred dog, given that it is a puppy: you must always take care of it, in any case, in any eventuality and, above all, it is a commitment that you must make for life of your dog! And there's no rain on this: as we often hear, in fact, you may have other dogs in your life, but a dog will only have you, so you need to take responsibility for keeping him healthy, educating him, but above all thinking about his well-being and his happiness! But our responsibility doesn't stop at this: having a dog also means having respect for the law. Why can't we let him roam around freely, allow him to attack other dogs, or even people. We therefore have the possibility of keeping him under control and training him so that our dog cannot harm things or people.

Basically, the owner of a dog is responsible for the well-being, control and management of his pet and is liable for damage or injury to people, other animals and things caused by the animal itself, even if it was lost or run away, unless it is not possible to prove the fortuitous case (unforeseen, unpredictable and inevitable event). This responsibility also extends to those who, although not the owner of the dog, have it with them or have it in their custody (responsible keeper).

Anyone who lets dangerous animals free, or does not keep them with due caution, or entrusts their custody to an unsuitable person (such as, for example, children or people unable to hold back a dog, should it become aggressive) risks an administrative fine. The same sanction is foreseen for those who incite or frighten animals, to endanger the safety of people. From the point of view of civil liability, compensation for damage caused by an animal can be requested by contacting the owner of the animal itself or the person who held it at the time of the events, if different. Knowing the rules that the law imposes, to walk or keep the dog safely, and respecting them every time you leave the house with him is essential to avoid dangerous situations or damage, but it is also important to ensure the well-being of the dog.

In fact, a well-guarded dog is less likely to cause damage, and, in parallel, the risk of suffering them is reduced.

This is to make you understand the full importance of training your dog correctly, from a puppy... and that's why we're here!

The benefits of owning a dog

Now that we have recognized our responsibility towards the possibility of owning a dog, let's briefly see what the benefits of adopting a puppy can be.

Especially for the little ones of the house, a dog can become an excellent example of life to follow: have you ever noticed how quickly and accurately he is able to bring back an object, as if it were a precious gift and just for you? And how can he keep the little ones under control by almost replacing the parent? For children there is only to learn and for adults only to observe and enjoy this special gift and relationship.

Discover then the main benefits of having a dog at home.

The dog is good for the health of the whole family

Several scientific studies have shown it: dogs at home are a guarantee of good health. In fact, they help reduce blood pressure and fight heart disease, decrease cases of depression among us humans and limit stress.

Because the dog at home is especially good for children

Those born and raised with a dog at home run less risk of suffering from allergies and asthma. Not to mention that they will then become excellent playmates! For the very little ones of the house who are learning to move in space and crawl or walk coordinating their steps for the first time, the presence of the dog is a continuous home stimulus to movement. The dog follows them, imitates them, encourages them and moves in front of them... moreover, it is the only one who sees the world at their level! A dog at home helps children improve their perception of themselves, elevating their ability to relate to others. He is also able to teach him responsibility: in daily care, for example, entrusting the child with some simple tasks concerning the dog's life.

The dog at home, a positive example of fidelity, responsibility and obedience

For older children, the dog's loyalty is an example of unprecedented loyalty and kindness. If the boy or girl is disappointed by a friend who has behaved badly and has moved away by betraying them, the fidelity with which the dog awaits the return of the family to the house every day is just one of the good examples that the dog is capable of teach to make them regain the right trust in others. When the dog quickly returns the ball to the master as if it were the most precious and desired object in the world, this is the best example of obedience that can be done and from which to learn. At that moment our four-legged friend teaches us that it doesn't matter what task is assigned, the important thing is to carry it out in the best way. A life lesson for humans of all ages, from those who have to do their homework in the afternoon to those who are learning a new job.

If you're a parent, how many times have you yelled for the toy chest to be put back or for help to set the table? Once again, the example of life can come right from the four-legged house: used to do his business at the right time and place, to bring his slippers back to his master, to wait for his food in an orderly bowl, he is a clear example of the sense of responsibility in daily household chores.

Helps stay fit and makes you happy!

A domestic dog is an exceptional personal trainer: at least three times a day it reminds you to exercise and doesn't skimp on sprints, jogs, quick walks, guaranteeing you perfect physical shape.

The magical symbiosis that is created between you and your dog is simple and genuine. Furthermore, it has been calculated that half an hour in the company of a four-legged is enough for us to feel joy and inner well-being grow.

Together is better

Family life with the presence of one or more dogs is a real inner enrichment for everyone. This is why it is important to learn to live peacefully, with immediate and lasting benefits.

Choosing the right breed for your lifestyle and home environment

The choice of dog, if you didn't know it, says a lot about us. When you choose to live with a furry friend, opting for a dog breed that reflects your personality in terms of characteristics can make living together easier and more natural. To every dog its owner and vice versa. Yes, because for each of us (it seems) there is an ideal dog. It's not an exact science, but it really seems that the choice of dog is guided by aesthetic and character analogies that assimilate masters and dogs, a bit like in the game of couples. Irony aside, personality, lifestyle and our habits are fundamental parameters on which to weigh the choice of the most suitable dog.

In fact, as we have seen just above in this chapter, adopting a dog is a choice of great responsibility which has innumerable practical implications. And if the fact that the various dog breeds differ in character and temperament is acceptable, it could be just as true that our way of being makes us more compatible with a Poodle rather than a Rottweiler.

Anyway, bringing a pet into your life is not an easy choice. For this reason, it is good to make sure of this decision and consider some factors to choose the right dog for your lifestyle.

So, if you are thinking about starting a cohabitation with a furry friend, it might be useful to reflect on some correlations between you and your potential best friend.

To choose the dog breed that best suits you, your home and your needs, know that there are specific tests online.

Let's be clear: there are no dogs more lovable than others, just as there are no people more capable and deserving of looking after a dog than others. Certainly, however, some distinctive personality traits can more or less happily unite different owners and breeds.

But, to give you some general guidelines here, here's how you can make this all-important choice.

The importance of size

It seems trivial, but one of the first parameters to consider when selecting a dog to adopt is its size. The puppy you see before your eyes will one day grow up and may outgrow the size of your apartment.

This will result in an unhappy and serene existence for both and will almost certainly cause continuous domestic disasters.

In any case, the size of the place where the dog will stay is the only important factor you should consider when choosing. One of this is if you live in a small apartment or a big house. Or the available space. It is important to consider all the needs of the various breeds for example, large breeds such as Great Danes can be more prone to physical ailments, such as hip problems. While smaller breed dogs like Chihuahuas can be more vulnerable to physical injury or colder temperatures than large breed dogs. Therefore, if the space that you can allocate to your dog is limited, the advice is to opt for small and medium-sized dog breeds with a calmer temperament. Miniature Pinscher, Pug, Pekingese, Pomeranian, Jack Russell, Beagle, Yorkshire, Maltese, Pekingese, and Shar Pei are just a few examples.

Beyond the space, it will be necessary to consider the character and habits of both. This will determine even more the compatibility between dog and owner and the empathy that will characterize their relationship.

Commitments

Choosing the type of dog that is compatible with your busy schedule will make you quite sure about the fact that your animal friend gets all the attention it needs. Do you have the free time to train a puppy properly? Will you be able to give an energetic dog with the long walks and activities he needs?

Activity level

Finding a beloved dog that matches with your activity level is vital when you are going to take a dog with you. A highly active dog can quickly exhaust a dog owner with a more sedentary lifestyle and vice versa. The best choice for you will be a dog whose needs are likable to yours. Based on your level of activity, races will be specified below in this regard.

Sports dogs

If you are an experienced runner and love exercise and outdoor activities, you will surely need a dog that can follow you on every outing. In general, shepherd or hunting dogs are the best companions for jogging, cycling, running or Nordic walking in the city and in the countryside. The Golden Retriever, the Poodle, the Border Collie, the Australian Shepherd and the Labrador Retriever, for example, love to run along the paths together with their owner, or in groups. They are very sociable, dynamic and resistant dogs, especially over short distances.

If the physical effort you dedicate to sport is even greater, the dog for you is the Jack Russel Terrier, but also the Bracco, the Fox terrier or the Dobermann. Remember that to play sports with a dog, it should be at least one year old, especially if they are medium-large sized dogs. Small dogs, on the other hand, can start as early as 8 months.

Dogs for lazy people

If sport isn't exactly your thing and you prefer to stay at home on the sofa lazing around, perhaps you should choose a dog who, like you, prefers a sedentary life. It being understood that dogs and owners still need to practice physical exercise at least twice a week, calmer personalities must be accompanied by equally seraphic 4-legged friends. In the ranking of the laziest dogs ever, the Bulldogs undoubtedly excel.

In particular, the French Bulldog, the English Bulldog and the Basset Hound seem to be born for relaxation. Were it up to them, they would spend the whole day dozing off, with brief breaks only for meals. The Pug is perhaps the laziest of the small dogs. When he sleeps, he snores loudly, and the bad news is that he loves to sleep very much.

Slightly more active, but without exaggerating, is the Dachshund who however also loves to dedicate some time of the day to play. But among the dogs that love tranquility and pampering there are also unsuspected 'giants'.

This is the case of the Newfoundland and the Saint Bernard who do not like movement, they suffer from the heat and much prefer a quiet walk to a jog.

Playful dogs

Lazy, active or just playful? If you recognize yourself in this last definition, the choice of the perfect dog could fall between one of these breeds. The Maltese is intelligent and lively, as are the Jack Russell and the Dalmatian. They are sociable dogs, always cheerful and strong-willed. They love any ball game and suffer tremendously from loneliness if the owner does not put them at the center of attention.

A bit like the Springer Spaniel, a relative of the English Cocker, who also loves to play with children. And how can we fail to mention the Boxer, a dog with a docile and amiable character, with an innate passion for play and the family towards which he shows boundless affection.

Dogs for adventurers

Are you a lover of adventure and risk? Are your passion excursions into unexplored territories and adrenaline? The most suitable dog for you, in this case, could be the German Shepherd. Strong and courageous like few others, it is safe to bet that he will follow you everywhere as a good and intrepid adventure companion.

Not least in terms of spirit of adventure is the Caucasian Shepherd who has an innate propensity for extreme situations and outdoor life. His motto is 'never back down in the face of difficulties'! Another dog breed that lends itself to long excursions is the German Bracco, formidable in hunting and a great walker.

Fatigue doesn't scare him and neither does danger. Another dog for real tough guys is the Bullmastiff, disruptive in size and temperament. To manage it you need physical strength and character firmness as it tends to overwhelm the master in every sense. Better to always keep him on a leash...

Last but not least intrepid is the Akita. He is the courageous dog par excellence but also a tough nut to crack to train. He loves walking along rough paths, he is a great hunter and has a very strong predatory instinct. A true adventure professional.

Race

Different breeds have different characteristics. Each breed has different personalities and it's important to know the right one that will be most compatible with your life. You can also consider that unknown mixed breed dogs may have all the ideal traits you are looking for, but you will never be guaranteed of it therefore, it will always represent an unknown quantity.

Age

Puppy, adult or senior: you should know that at every single stage, a dog's personality changes. When dealing with older dogs, you already know their medical history and personality, so the risk is lower than taking a younger puppy. However, some older dogs may not have been trained to work with young children (sometimes due to traumatic experiences in the past), so this is another important consideration. And for this reason, we have dealt with the training topic since we were puppies.

History

If you are buying the dog from a kennel, you will be able to learn about the history of the dog and its ancestors. If, on the other hand, you're adopting him from an animal shelter, his history may be less clear. It's enough thinking about the fact that this wonderful pet may have been abandoned or even abused and these events may have influenced his personality. However, even if with a difficult past, it's not said that he's not the perfect dog for you, but a little patience will just be needed to fit him into your life.

Preparing your home for a new dog

Are you ready to have a four-legged friend in your home? If yes, then it is massively advisable that you find out which breeds would not only match with your personality but with your lifestyle as well. You may be a true dog lover, but if you choose to take care of a dog that isn't right for you, then you and your dog aren't going to have much fun together. Taking care of a dog, we repeat once again, is a long-term commitment, so make sure you're ready for it.

But you have finally found your puppy and the whole family has literally fallen in love with him. And you are, precisely, willing to take responsibility for caring for this puppy in the long run.

Now we just have to wait until he's old enough to go home with you and start a new life together.

At the same time that you are waiting, there are some strategies you can do to make your home a safe and welcoming place for your new family member.

For your pup, leaving both mom and her playmates will be a big step, and it can be challenging times.

A good idea is to ask the breeder to leave something of yours inside his kennel (e.g., a shirt) so that he can get used to the smell of his new home and his new owners.

You can keep this process with making a "puppy proof" in your home. A new puppy, like a child, will start snooping around the house: that's why it's important to look at your home from his perspective. Behave with your new puppy as you would with a child, and you won't go wrong. Here's how to prepare for your new life together.

But what are the steps to follow before you bring your puppy home? Here's everything you need to arrange for the puppy:

Find a vet

When you get a dog it's a good idea to find out among your friends or in the neighborhood, to find a veterinary doctor close to home and immediately register at the clinic together with your puppy (if you don't already have another dog and therefore already have a doctor trusted veterinarian). It is best to be placed on the patient list as early as possible so that you can travel to the veterinary facility should any need arise.

Take out puppy insurance

While you're at the vet, ask if they can recommend puppy insurance policies that will cover any unexpected veterinary costs.

Find training courses

It's important that your new puppy is socialized and learns to relate, with other dogs and humans as well. And this is the aim of this guide: we will explain better in the next chapter, but here we tell you that your veterinary surgeon will be able to advise you on training courses for puppies and growing dogs. Lessons for puppies are a lot of fun and often friendships are born between various dogs and their owners that last a lifetime. I see this last part a little strong, I would remove it!

Order ID tag and microchip

You are legally required to place an identification tag on your dog's collar. In addition to the collar, the dog must have a microchip for its identification. The microchip is applied under the skin of the puppy by the veterinary surgeon; it's a painless surgery that takes seconds to perform. This procedure is required by law, so it's best to do it as soon as possible.

What to buy to welcome a puppy at its best

It's time to go shopping and put together everything you need to have at home to welcome the puppy. For this we have prepared you a complete list of everything. You will see, it will be a fun task and you will need a lot of willpower to stop yourself from buying the whole shop! Even if you feel tempted to buy a ton of toys for your pup's first day home, you should make sure you've covered the essentials first.

Here are all the essentials for your pup:

Two bowls

Make sure your puppy has a food bowl and a water bowl. They can be ceramic or stainless steel; they should be sized appropriately for the size of the puppy and easy to clean perfectly.

Leash and collar in nylon or leather

To help get your puppy used to walking on a leash and not pulling, you may want to get a gentle collar.

Grooming tools

You'll keep your pup nice and tidy with a complete grooming tool set that includes grooming mitt and gentle comb.

Some safe, fun and challenging toy

Be prepared to give your puppy good mental and physical exercise. There is a huge selection of toys that you can choose to use depending on your lifestyle. From interactive ones that hide a delicious snack inside to toys to be used in the garden that are used for practice and exercise, such as tunnels or jump rings. Remember that the veterinary doctor will be able to advise you on the games that best suit your four-legged friend's needs.

A kennel or bed

There is a wide choice of kennels and beds, it's up to you to find the one that best suits your puppy's size and temperament. Remember that some kennels are more indestructible than others! Whatever you choose, make sure it is in a warm, quiet place where there are no drafts.

A pet carrier, padded or wire mesh

Puppies especially love the security of the wire mesh kennel that they can turn into a den. These kennels can also help speed up the house-training process since puppies won't want to ruin their "special place".

Puppy food

Check what type of puppy food the breeder or shelter provided and ask your vet for advice.

How to "puppy-proof" your home and garden

Your pup's first few days at home will be one of constant roaming and sniffing as he explores his new environment. But that's exactly how many accidents and escape attempts also happen. Fortunately, there are some things you can do to limit the chances of unexpected events happening.

Here's how to puppy-proof your home and garden:

✓ Dedicate an area to the puppy.

The puppy needs a place of its own and that doesn't mean the whole house. Establish an area in your home that will temporarily become his "apartment". In this way the dog will not wander everywhere looking for things to chew and the probability of unpleasant incidents occurring is reduced to a limited area.

✓ Remove anything that is possibly risky to your health from your reach.

Plants, medicines and even household cleaning products can tickle the curious mind of a puppy who is learning about the world. Make sure they are placed where his little paws can't reach.

✓ Keep your favorite clothes and shoes in a closet.

Put away your precious shoe collection and make sure that the doors of the closets are closed tightly, to prevent your wardrobe from becoming a chew toy.

✓ Close the low windows of the house well.

Block off escape routes to ensure that the lively and inquisitive puppy can't get out.

✓ Make sure the garden fence is high enough.

It should be high enough to discourage your pup from any trips over the fence. Also check that there are no small gaps between the fence panels that your pup could escape through.

✓ Make sure your garden plants are dog friendly.

Some of the more common plants are to be avoided: lilies, tomatoes and daffodils.

What to do on the first day to welcome the puppy

The big day has arrived! Be sure to set aside some time to help your new furry friend get oriented and acclimate to his new abode.

There are a few other things you need to do after you bring your puppy home like:

✓ **Make time to settle your puppy.**

Allow enough time for the newcomer to acclimate to the new environment and establish a daily routine.

✓ **Choose his name.**

One of the many great things about having a dog is choosing the perfect name for him. In the moment you will choose a name you like, start using it as early immediately and every time you interrelate with the puppy. He will soon recognize it and start to come to you when you call your loved puppy!

✓ **Agree on a list of house rules.**

It is important for your puppy that every member of the family behaves consistently from the very first day at home. For example, if one family member allows him on the couch and another does not, this will confuse him. It is very easy for puppies to develop very cheeky habits if they are not kept in check. There are also certain rules to be set for human family members. If you know you have a puppy who likes to chew on things and you leave a pair of expensive trainers or a cell phone charger within reach, you're heading for trouble.

✓ **Keep calm.**

On the first day at home, it's very easy to shower your new dog with affection. Especially for younger family members. But while your new puppy is getting used to his new surroundings, it's important to supervise the over-enthusiasm of the children and give the dog time to settle in.

✓ **Invest your time well with the puppy.**

If you take time off work to settle your new puppy, make sure he is only home alone for short periods, but steadily increasing during the first week. You don't want your return to work to be a traumatic event for him, nor do you want your furniture chewed because your puppy is distressed, panicky, and suffering from separation anxiety.

If you're choosing a dog from a shelter, ask to the staff for having a general idea of any preferences or habits your new puppy may want.

Finally, keep in mind that when you bring your new puppy home, he may be a little overwhelmed by the excitement and changes he's going through, so it may seem a bit private at first. He will soon settle in and act like a member of the family, but if you notice he continues to stand aloof contact your vet.

✓ **Prepare a comfortable bed.**

To sleep peacefully, your new companion needs a bed, preferably washable. Get help from your children to place the bed in a warm, quiet place away from drafts. For puppies, the ticking of a clock or the soft sound of the radio can help them relax.

To sum up what we have said so far in this paragraph, after deciding on the type of dog that's right for you, all you have to do is buy everything you need to welcome the new member into your home (bowl, kennel, toys, leash and collar) and then go to the kennel or kennel to pick up the chosen dog and take it home with you. Afterwards, take him for a visit to your trusted vet to check his medical picture and carry out the necessary vaccinations. Choose the most suitable dog food based on its characteristics and manage its introduction to its new home in the best possible way.

Chapter 2: Puppy Training

Here we are in the second part of this book, the one in which we will talk about real puppy training. Puppy training is a critical component of raising a well-behaved dog. This chapter covers house training, basic obedience training (such as sit, stay, come), and socialization and exposure to different environments.

House training

Without a doubt, dogs are regarded as the ultimate companion animal. In order for their company to be as fun, pleasant and rewarding as possible, it will be necessary to train the dog Dogs are still today animals that let themselves be guided by their instincts, to avoid inappropriate or even unpleasant behavior during family life or a simple walk it will be necessary, even with the use of games, to educate the dog. The educational process and play are two important aspects of the puppy's growth phase. An educated and obedient puppy is more likely to grow into a balanced and serene adult dog.

When your puppy responds exactly to commands like "paw" or "sit" for the first time, his owner is bursting with joy and pride. Teaching your dog to respond to commands does not only mean having fun together, but also greater security during the daily routine. Light but effective training is important since your furry friend is still a puppy. To this end, you can choose

22

products for your house with different functions that can facilitate the training and training of your dog. They will help you achieve the first goals with ease and establish clear communication between you and the little puppy. Dogs are social animals, and it is such a natural thing. For this reason, for them, spending hours alone indoors could be a source of anxiety and stress for your pup. This condition could lead him to bark, soil or chew on objects. That's why it's important to educate and get your puppy used to spending time alone.

However, a puppy being brought home for the first time will need to be house trained. At the same time that you improve your patience skills, this is a huge chance to develop a bond with your new puppy.

Here are some useful little tips on training at home:

✓ Once of the certain thing for a puppy is socialization, that is, learning to relate to people, other animals and its environment. So, it must be interacting car noises, crowds of people, children, parks, etc. So, the tip is referred to expose your pet, in a natural manner, to everything that will be part of its entire life.

✓ He also needs to learn to calm down when petted. It is fundamental that the puppy feels your contact all over his body: belly, legs, but also ears. At the end you can give your 4 – legged friend a treat in the form of food. This could be a big learning motivation since puppies love food. To learn how to do your business outside the home, a good idea is to establish a routine of walking at the same time each time. You can say "no" in a firm voice if the puppy does his business at home, but only then, because dogs live in the present and not in what they have done in the past.

✓ Puppies know the world with their mouths and it's normal for them to bite. You could say "no" in a firm voice when your dog bites what you have in your hands. But, in this case, you can and give your puppy toys in return that he may bite.

Here is a routine scheme that you will need for home training:

1. Repetition

Engage in different activities at the same times each day – whether it's eating, walking or sleeping, it helps your puppy develop a routine.

2. Control

23

Keeping your puppy on a leash every time you take him outside to do his business helps prevent him from wandering off and starting to wander around getting distracted.

3. Consistency

Using the same simple command, such as "quick" or "toilet," just before the puppy starts to urinate, serves as a clearly recognizable cue for the puppy.

4. Reward

When your pup responds positively to new commands, give him a treat to let him know you approve.

Tools and equipment for puppies training

If a puppy has just joined your family, you're probably wondering how to train him. And right here, the big question arises: How to train my dog? To achieve this goal of being able to house train your puppy, you will need to have all the dog accessories you will need. With these and your patience you will succeed in turning your dog into the perfect pet. Among these tools we have:

Collars, muzzles and harnesses for training

The first step in educating your dog is to ensure that daily walks are cheerful and pleasant for both him and you. You can always find a variety of training collars online. Most of these come in the form of leashes and harnesses, so you can walk with your dog in perfect safety thanks to its anchoring/locking to the head, neck and chest.

At first glance they might seem a little complicated, but the manufacturers of this type of training collars design them in such a way that they are not only efficient but also comfortable for the animal. In fact, they serve to make the dog understand that he cannot constantly tug during a walk, but that he must learn to walk at the pace imposed by the owner, who is in charge in this relationship.

The different types of dog harnesses, with the passage of time and perseverance end up fulfilling their function of training your dog.

Dumbbells-weights for dogs

Although dog harnesses and collars are necessary tools for his education, it is equally true that dogs need to run free so that they can release all their energy, to feel healthy, strong and happy.

Nonetheless, these moments cannot be left without any kind of supervision, since nobody wants their dog to run away, cross the road or approach where it shouldn't. For this reason, the ideal would be to have this exercise done by playing with us.

In this sense, dog dumbbells are an excellent resource. If there is something that dogs love and that the master throws something that they can go crazy for running after it. Right here and where dumbbells come into play, with a variety of weights and materials, and with the shape specially studied by its specialized producers.

Dumbbells are both fun and educational for your dog. Since the goal is not for the dog to chase the fictitious prey but to bring it back afterwards. Once the dog understands that the game of coming and going and continues the work is done, it will be difficult for him to go out for a walk with him without his favorite handlebar.

Dog whistles and clickers

Another method of undisputed efficiency for dog education are whistles and clickers. Dogs' sense of hearing is not the same as humans, they have the ability to hear frequencies that are imperceptible to us. This is exactly where this type of whistle and acoustic elements come into action. Training with clickers and whistles, and some ultrasounds, serve to be aware when he has behaved well. If he obeys us or sits down at the indicated moment, the clicker sound will turn on and he will understand that he has respected the order (obeyed). He will eventually understand this if we additionally give him a dog treat as a reward.

Anti-bark collars and other systems to prevent the dog from barking

Whether your dog is small or large, what can annoy you most about him is hearing him bark. It's not easy to educate him not to do it, since barking, together with body language, is his main means of communication. Nonetheless, you have to teach him that he can't bark when he wants to.

For this reason, an effective tool is the anti-bark collar. These are collars with a built-in device that is activated with a remote control, so that when our dog barks and we want to let him know that he shouldn't, we cause him a thousand ampere discharge, so that he receives a corrective signal. They are not harmful to the animal at all, given that the current they receive is minimalThe manufacturers that offer this type of collars design them in such a way as not to cause any kind of trauma or pain to your dogs.

Another corrective method to prevent the dog from having it is for example the dog spray, to be used at the precise moment in which the dog barks or misbehaves.

Repellents and chase dogs

Even in spray format, the big brands in the pet industry offer their aerosols to prevent your dog from going to the toilet where he shouldn't. There are different types of dog repellent sprays, they can be used both inside the house and in the garden. So that by the smell that the sprayer gives off, the dog will know that he will never have to go near them to do his business.

There are other types of sprays, depending to the needs of our dogs as well, but we are specific talking about sexual needs. They are sprays designed to be sprayed on the female during the heat period, so that, by impregnating her, it causes the male dogs to move away. In this way it will be possible to avoid unpleasant behaviors, pregnancies and fights between males who want to mate with the female. This last item is not part of the training tools itself, however, it can prove extremely practical.

Basic obedience training (sit, stay, come, etc.)

Puppies have a remarkable learning ability. They can learn very quickly and have fun at the same time if the educational session is well organized. Teaching basic commands can make him more comfortable in social contexts and easier to manage. In addition, it also helps to ensure its safety in highly frequented or dangerous places. As a result, you will have the possibility to take him anywhere and meet whoever you want with complete peace of mind. The tabs below list some of the essential daily commands you'll need:

- ✓ **Sit**
- ✓ **Stay on the ground**
- ✓ **Wait**
- ✓ **Come to you**
- ✓ **At the foot**

Let's see how you can teach your puppy each of these individual commands.

How to teach a puppy to sit

Start by holding a snack in front of the puppy's face. As he lifts his head to follow the treat, your dog should naturally sit up. When the action is over, give him the treat and pet him.

It will be necessary to repeat these steps several times for the puppy to learn to associate the reward with the act of sitting. Afterwards, continue making the same hand gesture, but gradually cut out the snack. In the moment your dog gets used to it, you can put a verbal cue too.

How to teach your puppy to lie down

As soon as your puppy has learned how to sit, the moment of teaching it to lie down is coming. You can teach this command by holding a treat, lowering it between his front paws and pulling it away. When the puppy can do it, reward. Keep repeating these steps, gradually cutting out the treat, until your puppy is able to end the action in any time.

At this point, you can also begin to associate a verbal cue with the command.

How to teach a puppy to wait

Start by making your dog sit with a wave of the hand and saying the word "Sit". Put your hand in front of you, palm forward, saying the word "Stay"!

So, now you should attend a few seconds, then reward your dog if he stays still. So, repeat the exercise. Have the dog perform the "Sit," but this time step back with your palm facing the dog and say the command, "Stay." Wait a few seconds, then step forward and reward him.

Repeat these steps gradually increasing the amplitude of the step back, giving your dog a reward each time he performs the command. Remind to "release" your dog once each exercise is finished, by encouraging him to stand up. You will find that frequent sessions of several minutes will yield better results.

How to teach your puppy to come to you

Puppies cannot hold attention for long, so it is advisable to organize these teaching sessions in a quiet area with very few distractions. The first step is to be letting your puppy walk away, then squat down, open your arms and employ a sort of excited tone of voice to say his name. And this should be followed by the word you use as a signal. When he arrives, pet him, compliment him, or reward him with a treat. Then, give him another snack while you put his leash on. Once the snack is finished, unhook the leash, stand up and walk away. Now start again with the same steps.

You should do it every day for a few weeks, in short sessions.

How to teach the puppy to come "heel"

Start by seating your puppy. Place a snack in your hand and hold it level with his muzzle. Then walk forward quickly and say "foot."

When your dog is about to walk up to you, stop and make him sit. It's time to reward him and repeat these steps for some other minutes.

Exercise with your puppy whenever you have the opportunity. This command is not easy to learn, and the dog learns it late in his teaching process. It will therefore be important to dedicate frequent sessions for a certain period of time.

Socialization and exposure to different environments

More than anything, dogs want to make you happy, which is why they are almost always easily trainable. Before you begin, make a list of the basic commands you want to teach him: "sit", "stay", "come", "down" or "no" (which always comes in handy). It would also be advisable to teach him to stop barking on command, not to beg for food and not to dirty the house. All of this is perfectly doable and just requires persistence, praise, the occasional food reward, and lots of patience and positivity.

Useful tips

Here is a list of useful things to know when deciding to expose your puppy to different environments:

✓ Choose the most suitable puppy for you. The first fundamental thing is to choose a dog that suits you, your lifestyle and your family. After having identified the breeding or the litter from which you want to take your dog, it is advisable to proceed in choosing the puppy carefully based on its specific character.

✓ Try to gradually get him used to being alone. The dog is perfectly capable of getting used to being alone for some periods of time, but it is obviously necessary to make a gradual transition from a condition of community life to a condition in which we will ask to spend time independently.

✓ Once you get home, always remember that it's important for the puppy to play. It is an activity that must be managed with frequent but short-lived phases, without tiring him too much and trying to understand his reactions to stimuli.

- ✓ Get him a suitable place to rest. The puppy initially spends several hours of the day resting, in these moments it is better to leave him alone or to devote himself to calming activities.
- ✓ Get your new friend used to doing his needs outside right away. You can do this by giving the dog the opportunity to go out regularly and rewarding him when he gets dirty outside. Positive reinforcement is key.
- ✓ Maintain puppy safety. Before the arrival of the puppy, it is best to remove all objects that could easily nibble or ingest from the dog's reach. Any small or angular object could be a potential danger.
- ✓ So, give the right rhythms to his day. The puppy sleeps a lot but also needs to carry out activities. Program for him short but intense moments of play, cuddles, discovery of the house, relationship with the other pets, etc. Don't wait for the puppy to activate, he would always do it when you're busy with something else and this would put you in difficulty.

Don't neglect your dog's education. To better enjoy the relationship with him and allow you to take him in any situation, it is advisable to involve him in a program designed around his needs.

How to educate him not to dirty at home

When training a puppy not to soil in the house, early "accidents" are inevitable, so arm yourself with patience and optimism. This is one of the fundamental things you may teach to your dog, and the first thing to do is establish a routine. Dogs are creatures of habit, so schedule specific moments for his hygienic walks: after he has eaten, played or slept, before putting him in the kennel and every time you see him sniffing around looking for a place to urinate. When he does his business in the right place, reward him with lots of praise. Even a snack given immediately afterwards will motivate him to repeat the correct behavior the next time. Over time your puppy will learn where and when to litter. But remember that not all puppies are perfect, and you may have to clean up some minor mess.

How to get your puppy dirty outside when you live in the city?

Did you know that most dogs find it very difficult to get dirty in the city when they are puppies? It happens because the dog as a puppy, while dirty, feels vulnerable and for this reason he doesn't feel safe getting dirty in crowded and noisy places.

In our daily work we have to find easy solutions to help the dog adapt to any environment. Here is a little trick divided into 4 steps that you can use immediately to train your puppy to dirty outside the home:

1- Always choose a quiet place, sheltered from traffic and the comings and goings of people.

2- Stop for a few minutes and give yourself time to feel safe.

3- Reward him a lot with caresses when he gets dirty.

4- Once you have identified the dog's favorite quiet place, where it gets dirty in a short time, always bring it back there initially. Puppies tend to always dirty in the place where they recognize their smell, which makes them feel safer.

Follow these steps and you will see that your puppy will soon get used to dirtying outside the house. Training a puppy to go outside requires perseverance: don't forget this.

How to teach puppy to socialize

Socialization with other dogs from an early age is vital important. This way you will always make him happier, and he will not develop problems in adulthood. Socialization is in fact the learning process through which puppies get used to become close to different people, animals and environments. Suitable socialization can be useful to remove some behavior problems in the future. Not only for this: one socialization purpose is to give birth to a better bond between the puppy and the family.

In fact, it does not escape the fact that when puppies are introduced to new people, other pets or new environments, the puppy is allowed to have a positive experience, reacting to every new stimulus and thus improving its personality.

Of course, while the socialization process should start as early as possible, don't forget that you shouldn't introduce your puppy to other dogs until he has been properly vaccinated, and that you should always consult your veterinarian to determine when your puppy is ready to share spaces with other dogs.

The best way to create socialization is to expose your puppy to as many people, places and animals as possible. There are dogs that are afraid of bearded men, or people who wear gloves, while others are terrified of getting into a car or bark furiously at their own kind. These eccentricities of character can be remedied with socialization, especially when the dog is young. Anyway, always keep in mind 3 very important concepts that all owners should know:

- ✓ **Guide the dog in experiences.**
- ✓ **Progression in difficulty.**
- ✓ **Dogs see things differently than we do.**

So, start by familiarizing the puppy with you and with your "touch". This will make it easier for you to trim your nails, brush your teeth, clean your ears, and administer medications.

For each dog, the process of approaching individuals and situations depends on the experiences lived at an early age and on his individual character. We must then relate it to the environment in which we live (city, countryside, mountains) and to the lifestyle we will have with the dog (very routine life, dynamic life with constant changes of situations, etc.).

In general terms, to train a puppy, the following must be "presented":

- ✓ **People of different ages, genders or ethnic groups.**
- ✓ **Animals that frequently live in the living environment of the dog (cats, birds, horses).**
- ✓ **Ordinary situations of city life (cars, mopeds, bicycles, public transport, public places, shops, shopping centers).**
- ✓ **Situations related to the house (stairs, lift, shared spaces).**

He must be able to know everything he will have to come into contact with growing up, but in the correct way for his well-being.

As a puppy, a dog learns what others in his pack are doing. There is quite a training program in the wild if you think about it: puppies have to learn how to get food (they learn to hunt).

It is also in fact important that the puppy learns to be comfortable with other animals. So, try to gradually expose your pet to other puppies, as long as they are vaccinated. This is why it is important to use specialized facilities at this stage, thus avoiding taking the puppy to a dog park or other public area until it has been adequately vaccinated. A puppy's exposure to infectious diseases, such as parvovirus, when his immune system is still developing, can unfortunately have very serious results.

Finally, we remind you that a useful way to socialize is to familiarize the puppy with all the sights and sounds of his world, from going to the car to being in the rooms while you are vacuuming. Once your puppy has been properly vaccinated, you can then take him to places like a park and grooming facility or expose him to other situations that have radically different sights, sounds and smells for him.

With advice on puppy socialization concludes our first book. Next we will focus on adult dog training.

BOOK 2: DOG TRAINING (ADULT)

Introduction

In this second book training focus will move on the adult dog.

In the last book, we talked about how it is possible to train a puppy.

In this one, however, we will deepen the discussion regarding an already grown dog. First of all we tell you that the arrival of a new four-legged member in the family is always an exciting moment, but there is a certain difference between adopting an adult dog and bringing home a puppy.

A dog who is no longer very young may have spent a rather long period in another house, or have lived in a kennel, so it may take him a while before he gets used to a new context and takes on new habits. If you are wondering how to train an adult dog, know that there are many things you can do to facilitate his training and help him settle in. And in this guide, through the 3 chapters of which it is composed, we will explain how to do it.

Chapter 1: Adult Dog Training

Once a dog reaches adulthood, there are different training techniques and skills to focus on. This chapter covers advanced obedience training (such as heel, down), addressing behavioral issues (such as barking, chewing, aggression), and agility and other forms of physical exercise.

Is it possible to train an adult dog? Tips and tricks

At this point, the first question you are asking yourself is whether it is possible to train an adult dog. But before answering this question, let's take a step back and ask ourselves: what is meant by an adult dog? What is their behavior? Dogs over the age of seven are considered senior (depending on the breed), which means you can live happily together for many more years! Whether you've chosen to adopt a dog from a shelter or have taken in a friend's dog, giving a large adult puppy a new home will do both you and him much good as your relationship develops.

The average life expectancy of a dog is about 12 years (small breeds tend to live longer than large breeds).

Adult dogs have an already consolidated character and (hopefully!) should have already learned to recognize some basic commands, such as the classic "sit", and have already been trained. However, as a new home arrives and a new routine and new expectations set in, it's important to support your puppy by continuing to educate him.

Dogs can learn at any age, so you can teach even an adult a few new tricks! So, even if training is usually associated with puppies and younger dogs, education is essential at any age.

Not surprisingly, adult dogs are easier to educate than puppies, as they get more self-control. Training a dog throughout his life will help keep him mentally stimulated and will strengthen your bond.

How to train an adult dog, 9 tips

Here you are 9 tips and tricks very useful for training your adult dog:

1. **Establish a routine and help your dog settle in**

Teaching your big dog when to expect meals, pee breaks, physical activity, playtime and bedtime is the key to getting him started to get to know the new routine and how the day will evolve.

Regular exercise must be an important part of this routine; in this regard, take into consideration the age of the dog and the intensity of the physical activity he needs – if you are not sure ask your vet. More frequent but short walks may be more suitable; Additionally, you may want to take your furry friend swimming, as swimming is great low-impact exercise.

2. Give your four-legged friend some time to get used to it

Remember to give your furry friend time to get used to his new home. He may need to stay in a quiet corner for a while, so make sure he has an area of his own or a kennel where he can rest undisturbed.

Create for him a comfortable bed full of soft cloths, with the bowl of water placed immediately next to it and some toys to have fun with.

If you use a crate, be aware that some dogs like to have a sheet placed on top, so they feel more secure. It is also worth checking if there is another area of the house that the dog has chosen and in which he spends a lot of time. It could be that this is his favorite corner and is therefore a perfect place to place the doghouse.

3. Support your dog with the use of a suitable dog diffuser

Wherever you decide to create a special space for your dog, consider using a suitable diffuser for dogs that will help him stay calm and better adapt to his new life. This tool will also provide him with support in the face of new situations he may encounter, such as being alone at home, hearing sudden noises, receiving guests or feeling afraid.

4. Educate him to do the needs in the right place

Most adult dogs have already been trained in their needs. However, since your four-legged friend has just been introduced to a new routine, at first, you'll want to give him a good understanding of where he needs to do them, just as you would with a puppy. Take him out regularly – for example after he has eaten and drunk, as well as after playing or exercising. Make sure you reward him right away when he does his business outdoors. Know when he needs to go out: for example, if you see him sniffing the floor, spinning around or heading for the door – and take him outside, always praising him and rewarding him when he does well.

5. Schedule regular training sessions

A fundamental point among the advice on how to educate an adult dog is to schedule training sessions on a regular basis. Passing some time together will strengthen your bond and will be useful for understanding each other better. Short 10-minute sessions will work great, and as with any dog, proceed with training when both you and him are calm and free from distractions. Remember that an adult dog may need more repetition than a puppy to learn new things, but the good news is that your friend will probably have a shorter attention span, so you should have more time before he starts to get distracted.

6. Consider getting professional training

Consider taking your dog to a training class to reinforce some basic commands, review walking on a leash, and facilitate his socialization with other dogs and other people in a safe environment. If your dog has difficulty with basic commands or has behavior problems, seek advice from a qualified behaviorist - the center where you adopted him could for example recommend a professional who is right for you. Contact your vet as well, to rule out any health issues.

Be patient!

For those who want to know how to educate an adult dog, we remind you that you must first of all be patient - your new life partner may need some more training before being able to learn something new, so be understanding. Repetition is key. Try moving the training to different locations once he has mastered everything perfectly around the house.

Make sure you abide by the rules right from the start. Everyone in the family must follow them, so that the dog understands what the expectations are (for example if he is allowed to get on the sofa or not). If the rules change for different people, it might just get confusing. Also make sure that everyone uses the same terms when giving commands so that your big puppy learns the behavior easily.

7. Never punish him

Using positive reinforcement is the best way to train your dog and will help you bond even more. When you want to reward him for good behavior, choose treats, praise or something special that you know your four-legged friend appreciates. This will make him understand that by behaving well he will achieve positive results. You may have to try several things before you find out what his favorite treat is! The shelter, or the person he previously lived with, may be able to suggest the most appropriate ways to encourage your big puppy. But it is vital that you never punish him: this fact can ruin your relationship and confuse him. This will be discussed later in this book.

8. Mix it up

Training moments spent learning new things can be a lot of fun for both you and your dog, so challenge yourself with different activities. For example, try a scent game to get him used to using his nose. Or consider filming yourself while you train: this is a great way to monitor the progress of training but also to keep track of the development of your friendship and see how your big puppy changes over time!

However, know that if you adopt an adult dog, don't be frightened by what you hear around: re-education is possible. The adaptation of dogs from one year of age onwards is helped by the gratitude that each specimen feels for the human who took him from the kennel. The dog is also a sociable animal, naturally inclined to quickly learn the rules of the group to which it belongs.

Advanced obedience training (heel, down, etc.)

At this point, first the re-education, then the advanced education of your adult dog begins. The first commands that the pack leader (you) will practice giving will be simple and direct: "stand up, sit down, stop, come" and so on. If the dog has difficulty understanding, be patient as he may have a very different past history and not very compatible with the present one. But if you can win his trust, he will soon go out of his way to please you and communication difficulties will soon become a thing of the past. The secret is to persevere. The most used method is always that of requesting and rewarding food or affection, which will lead you to progressively obtain the execution of increasingly complex commands. If, on the other hand, the dog performs an action that you don't want to repeat, ignore him and leave him alone for a few minutes.

If, on the other hand, you have taken a dog as a puppy and want to give it more advanced training, here's what you need to do!

How to teach to sit or go down

Unlike "Sit", with the command "Dock!" or "Down!" the dog should lie on the spot. Instead, saying "Down!" the animal is asked to go to its place, at home. When it is in the "Dog!" or "Down!", the dog's back and both elbows are on the ground. You can teach him this position by holding a snack right in front of his nose while in the "Sit!" and from there moving the hand slowly towards the ground, making the dog follow the movement with his eyes.

Keep the snack as parallel to the floor as possible. To get the coveted reward, the dog will go down with his muzzle first. Then slowly pull your hand away from his muzzle, keeping it above

38

the floor. He will follow your hand until he is "forced" to lie down in place. At that point he utters the command "Dog!" and give him his reward.

Before standing up, your dog should always "Sit!" at your command. Once your dog is seated, you can repeat or stop the exercise. There are many possible situations to practice the "Dock!" or "Down!" whatever you want: for example, at the bar, at the bus stop, during a casual conversation with a neighbor or later when you take him with you to the restaurant.

Again, timing is important: the more tired your dog is, the more willing he will be to lie down. So at first it is advisable to practice with the command "Down!" or "Dog!" after a long walk and not before, especially if you realize that your faithful friend is still full of energy.

Command "Let's go!" or "Foot!" or "Keep up!"

In heavy traffic, in crowded pedestrian areas or when meeting other dogs, it helps if your pet keeps pace reliably and calmly. This implies that with the command "Let's go!" (or "Foot!" or "Al pace!" if you prefer) the animal remains close to the owner walking sideways to its human. This must happen regardless of whether you go slowly or briskly, go straight ahead, turn or stop.

Traditionally the dog walks on his left side but of course you can also get him used to being on your right if you prefer. The important thing is that you, as far as possible, always keep the same side. Start the exercise by showing your dog a snack that you will be holding on the side you have chosen. As soon as the dog assumes the correct position, say the command.

Has a further signal, this time of a visual type, it is good that you clap your hand on your thigh, obviously from the side where the dog is walking. After a few meters, give the command "Sit!" and reward him with the snack. Over time you can make the exercise a little more challenging by inserting more and more turns or changes of direction.

You should also gradually push the treat away from his snout – for example, you can put the treat in his pocket and continue walking. At times you can go slower, or faster, sometimes turn right, left, go back... repeating the acoustic command "Let's go!" at each change. and the related visual signal. Only when your dog has learned to walk reliably and safely by your side can you repeat the exercise without a leash. If after taking the leash off your dog walks away, do not pull him by the collar but rather put the leash back on calmly and repeat the training from before, i.e., keeping the dog on the leash.

The Leave command

When you say, "Let go!", your dog should immediately let go of an object or whatever he's grabbed in his mouth. If, for example, your paw friend has gotten hold of a shoe or is holding a toy of your children in his mouth, you should clearly give him the command "Let go!" to let him know that you don't want him to.

first of all, it is necessary that the dog knows the basic command "sit"; this will be the starting point.

Get something that he can perceive as a reward worth doing something about: bites are certainly great to start with, allowing for immediate and quick gratification. For this type of exercise, they are perfect to hide in the hands.

How to teach to "heel"

It is very important to use a short command thus avoiding long sentences that can distract the dog from the request, a strong but friendly tone of voice and to involve our four-legged friend in the most stimulating way. Let's see together how to do it in detail.

✓ Take a good number of mouthfuls, so as to have the possibility of rewarding it several times and repeating the exercise easily, without having to interrupt it to look for new rewards.

✓ Have your dog sit across from you and grab his attention so he knows you've been working together ever since.

✓ Put a morsel in your hand, make a fist and give the command "paw" with a firm tone.

✓ Now you have to observe his reaction. Most likely he will lick your hand, sniff it or try a muzzle approach; in this case, remain unmoved and do not reward the dog, even if he has shown interest in the reward. Remember that the goal is to get your hand to touch his paw! If the dog instead tries to approach with a paw, then reward him by opening your hand, giving the bite and praising him verbally. If you both already know how to use the clicker, now is the right time to use it.

✓ What if the dog gets distracted? It means that he is not attracted enough to what you are doing or how you are presenting yourself. Try to get his attention better and repeat the exercise again.

✓ Arm yourself with patience! Exactly, in the recipe book of good dog education this is the main ingredient. Do not punish or scold the dog if it does not perform the exercise correctly.

In education with positive reinforcement, correct behaviors are rewarded and those that are not requested or performed in the wrong way are never punished. This approach will make you much more attractive to your dog and will keep them in the right frame of mind to work with, without fear or fear.

✓ Once the dog has learned to execute the "paw" command in this way, he moves on to a slightly higher level of difficulty, trying to perfect the exercise. The goal is to be able to get the paw by holding the hand with an open palm, without a reward in the fist. Offer the open palm to the dog, give the command and as soon as he has placed his paw in your hand, reward quickly, with your free hand, giving the bite and praising him.

In conclusion of this paragraph, we tell you to try not to have too long or insistent educational sessions because the dog could get bored, remember to always use the same command and not to use synonyms so that he is able to memorize a single word by associating it in the correct way with the action you are requesting.

Have fun together with your dog and remember that fun training is more stimulating for both of you.

Addressing behavioral issues (barking, chewing, aggression, etc.)

Now let's see how it is possible to address some possibly incorrect behaviors of our adult dog.

41

If you have decided to take in a dog that has developed serious behavioral problems, you need to arm yourself with a lot of patience. The most relevant critical point is that the adult dog has assimilated a certain behavior for months if not for years: if suddenly that usual behavior is perceived as undesirable, this generates stubbornness and insecurity in the dog. Changing a behavior that has already been learned requires a lot of effort on the part of the adult dog and therefore a lot of consistency and above all patience on the part of its owner. But, before you start "counteracting" the unwanted behavior with targeted training, you need to research the cause. Why is my dog having destructive behavior? Why is he reacting aggressively? Why doesn't it stop barking? Behind the biting and destroying act of some dogs there are mostly serious mental disorders that can be triggered not only by traumatic experiences, by living with chronic pain, but also by a strong uninterrupted state of stress, by a previous condition isolation or a protracted absence of physical and mental stimulation.

The more you know the causes of your paw friend's behavior, the more targeted and potentially effective you can make training your adult dog. In this type of situation, especially newbies, i.e. those who have no experience with dogs, should definitely look for an expert aim. But even for people who already have previous experience with dogs, a discussion with a dog trainer who is an expert in canine psychology and a visit to a dog school can prove useful and appropriate. In any case, below we will try to give you some general guidelines.

If the dog is aggressive

A dog can have various reasons for becoming aggressive: wrong education, strong insecurity, but also a simple tendency to be predominant. This is the case of the animal that does not accept to be subordinated to its master and that wants to decide independently on all fronts: from the game to the moment of needs.

This type of dog will try, through aggressive attitudes, to gain respect and if you don't firmly re-establish your role as leader, he will not respect you. How to do? Surely the right answer is not force because for the animal it would become a challenge to which it cannot say no, but to act with firmness and charisma. If the task proves too difficult, the advice is to contact professional trainers.

If the dog proves insecure

An insecure dog, if left alone, becomes restless, fears that his human companion has abandoned him and can cry, bark, dirty and bite everything. Changing his behavior means working hard and long on his self-esteem as the animal needs to regain trust in the world. The subject is vast but in general it can be said that the insecure dog should not be spoiled with too much attention and concessions. On the contrary, it is necessary to establish certain and strict rules to cling to. Your job will be to show him the way to overcome dangers, pains and stresses, not to avoid them. As in the education of the child, even in that of the dog it is counterproductive to pamper for no reason, to reward for no reason, to protect excessively.

Teach your adult dog to properly bark

Another important fix is to teach your dog to bark, or rather, to bark only when it's okay to do so. The first step in tackling the problem is to see why your dog is barking. Some dogs bark to show they want something. Maybe they're hungry, thirsty, or just want to play.

When this behavior becomes unreasonable, it's time to teach him other ways to get your attention; for example, by holding out the paw or waiting at the door or in front of the bowl. As second step, You need to simulate a situation where you know your dog is barking, and when he starts barking, tell him "bark" and make a hand gesture. When the 4-legged stops barking, give him a treat and say bravo. Keep practicing this exercise until your dog barks at your "bark" even without the need for external stimulation.

Now, introduce the word "stop": start by saying "bark" to your dog and, while he is barking, introduce the word "stop". When he stops barking, reward him. Then start gradually decreasing the number of rewards. Another way to teach your dog to shut up at your command is to distract him whenever he barks. Use something very loud, like a can full of coins, to get his attention, and then say the command "silence" very firmly.

Once stops barking, it's time to reward your dog. Never raise your voice when you want him to stop. This could cause anxiety and impair learning. It's also possible that he gets confused if he thinks you're "barking" too. Yelling only reinforces the barking habit.

Now try practicing this pattern in different situations. When the dog has learned the command at home, he starts practicing it outside (for example at a friend's house or in the park). This will help reinforce the learning. In case, however, your dog barks when he is home alone. Try leaving some music or a radio with familiar noises. A good way to reduce anxiety is to give your dog a piece of unwashed cloth or anything that still smells like his family.

When you get home, spend as much time with him as possible, let him play and exercise. He'll miss you, and there's no better way to reconnect.

At the end, one of the most common reasons dog barks is alarm. Once the dog watch someone approaching the house, he will bark to make you aware of it. Since he recognizes you as the boss, he will push you to investigate the potential danger. Some dogs have been trained to raise the alarm and you may want this behavior to be encouraged. So, let your dog bark for having your attention, but silence him if you realize there are no intruders.

How to train an adult dog not to bite

If when your dog grows up it doesn't stop biting everything, or you have simply taken on an adult dog with this vice, then it is essential to intervene because this behavior could even end up representing a risk or danger to other dogs or people. If the reason isn't due to a particular reason, then it could mean that your dog may be in pain somewhere in his body. If his paw hurts or he has been hit on the side, it will not be very pleasant for him to be touched on a part of the body that is inflamed. Especially if your dog has never done it before, biting you is his signal to let you know that he is in pain in that precise spot. Another reason could be attributable to a former violent owner: it is normal for a dog that has been subjected to violence by a man now to be wary and have the instinct to defend himself. In these cases, it is fundamental that you enlist the help of a veterinary behaviorist. Our advice is to entrust yourself to a dog trainer who will be able to educate your dog not to bite. Compared to managing a puppy, in fact, trying to educate an already adult dog is more complex since the dog will have internalized this behavior as normal. In general, remember that the most effective way to punish a dog for biting is to ignore him and not react so as not to reward his behavior with your attention. Conversely, if he behaves correctly, he uses positive reinforcement as an incentive to stop biting.

Agility and other forms of physical exercise

We conclude this chapter with some physical exercises, such as those helpful to develop your adult dog's agility. Exercise is essential for all adult dogs, but the intensity and duration of this activity will depend on their age, size and physical characteristics. Training your dog will help prevent obesity problems, lower stress levels and keep him happy and lively.

We will then give you some basic advice such as whether it should be practiced before or after eating or what is the correct intensity level for a dog practicing agility.

Benefits of exercise and basic advice

Animating your dog to exercise or better yet to exercise with him brings with it a number of health benefits for both of you. You should know that exercises are ideal for dogs suffering from stress or behavior problems in general, as it helps them release accumulated tension.

In addition, exercise is a way of preventing dog obesity, a fairly common and frequent problem. Keeping your dog away from being overweight also means helping him not to get arthritis, osteoarthritis or dysplasia. Although these diseases usually develop in old age, on occasion they can also occur in young dogs, but with excessive weight. Spending time with your dog exercising outdoors also helps him relate to the environment, dogs and other people.

If your dog isn't used to exercise you don't have to force him and demand a lot right away. It must be a gradual process in which he is the protagonist: the goal and also to entertain him. Before doing exercises, we have to walk quietly with our dog so that he does his needs so we don't have to stop and change the pace constantly.

It is very important to keep in mind that our pet should not exercise if he has just finished eating, it is better to feed him afterwards to avoid gastric torsion.

Choose a time of day that is conducive to exercise, such as at sunrise or maybe at sunset. Avoid times of day when it is very hot, it is important to avoid the possibility of heat stroke.

Finally, it is advisable to give him exercise in a quiet and safe place, where the dog feels comfortable.

Even if there are exercises in which we do not actively participate, we must keep in mind that our pet is happy if we exercise with him, therefore it is advisable to try to be as involved as possible. If we don't do this, it is possible that he will get tired of exercising in a short time.

Take extra care if your dog belongs to one of these breeds, as he should get moderate exercise. Some examples are:

- ✓ **Boxers**
- ✓ **Pug**
- ✓ **Rottweilers**
- ✓ **Dogue de Bordeaux**
- ✓ **Bullmastiff**
- ✓ **English bulldog**

Jogging with the dog

If you like running and your four-legged friend doesn't despise it either, you can start jogging with him. You won't need many things: a pair of shoes, a leash (unless you want to let it loose) and a large, safe place. Jogging, in general, is one of the best exercises for dogs.

Here you are some advice to follow with jogging dogs:

✓ **Check his paw pads frequently to make sure they aren't damaged.**

✓ **Especially in the case of dog crossing (we will explain what is immediately below), take several precautions to prevent your dog from getting heatstroke.**

✓ **He always carries a bottle with you, hydration is essential.**

✓ **Adapt your dog's diet to its level of physical activity.**

✓ **Visit the vet regularly to make sure all is well.**

✓ **Adapt the pace and duration to his abilities.**

Dog crossing

Dog crossing is a very complete exercise for tireless dogs that allows you and your pet to run together linked by a leash. It is ideal for dogs that need to get a lot of exercise but remember that they will need gradual training which will allow them to build muscle mass and stamina.

At a competitive level it is advisable to carry out a veterinary check before subjecting him to great efforts such as those of intensive dog crossing.

Cycling with the dog

Cycling is a fun and suitable sport for active but obedient dogs, with this type of activity we make him exercise actively in the city, mountains or other places, without getting excessively tired.

Remember that it is essential that your dog is obedient and understands basic commands such as "stop", "let's go", "right", "left". It is essential in order not to have an accident.

If you are wondering how to teach your dog to follow you while riding a bicycle, we offer you a simple step-by-step method that you will need to practice for some time before starting with this practice:

- ✓ **Show your dog the bike if he's never seen it before, let him smell and observe it for a while.**
- ✓ **Buy an adapter that connects the bike to the leash.**
- ✓ **Start a bike ride with the dog on a leash without getting on the bike, pushing it manually.**
- ✓ **When the dog feels comfortable, mount the saddle and start pedaling at a moderate speed.**

The agility dog

Approaching dog agility, whether at a competitive level or not, is a wonderful way of teaching him obedience and exercising your dog in an active way, in fact it is a very complete sport that can even be played at home or in a villa if you have enough space available. It is indicated for curious, agile dogs with good memory such as Border Collies.

Agility consists of an obstacle course that the dog must follow and overcome. The circuits include walkways, tunnels and wheel tires.

Swimming and hydrotherapy

As with people, taking your dog swimming in the ocean or pool is a great way to get them exercise in a fun way. To do this, our dog must be a water lover, if not, it is better to consider another sporting option. In this specific activity we will have to take safety measures to avoid possible drowning or gastric torsion, which can happen if we have recently fed him. Therefore, always pay attention to your dog. On the other hand, hydrotherapy is perfect for dogs suffering from muscle problems, injuries, dislocations, dysplasia, arthritis or osteoarthritis, as it helps them exercise without feeling pain.

Here some tips for swimming dogs:

- ✓ **Swimming is one of the best and most strenuous exercises, so hydrate your dog often.**
- ✓ **If your pet needs to start swimming on a regular basis, you should consider supplementing his diet with a more complete diet.**
- ✓ **Watch his paws so that they don't stay wet for a long time, otherwise they could develop fungus or other infections.**

With dog physical exercises we conclude our first chapter.

In the second we will talk about socialization and training for specific dog breeds.

Chapter 2: Socialization and Training for Specific Breeds

Different breeds have different training and socialization needs. This chapter covers special considerations for training and socializing certain breeds (such as working dogs, toy breeds), and tips for addressing breed-specific behavior traits.

Special considerations for training and socializing certain breeds (e.g., working dogs, toy breeds, etc.)

We make some special considerations based on the type of adult dog breed you have adopted or raised. Know, in general, that the easiest dog breeds to train are:

1. BORDER COLLIE

We are talking about of one of the most energetic pets ever. Not only this: border collie are also very obedient and loyal to his owner, practically anything he tells him he interprets it as an absolute law! Being basically very intelligent, he is able to store all the commands from an early age and understand what is asked of him. The Border Collie is also great at dog agility games and competitions!

2. POODLE

In the small barrel there is good wine! This is precisely the case of the Poodles, apparently vainer than anything else, instead they are educated dogs and attentive to learning what humans teach them. For the reason they are mad about company, they do everything to never be alone, so they somehow adapt and indulge in the requests of their owners.

3. GERMAN SHEPHERD

Genetics is definitely an important trait that affects how easy a dog is to train. When it comes to deal with loyalty and fidelity towards its owner the German Shepherd are unique in the world; he is an athletic, agile dog, prone to learning and easy to train for any task.

4. GOLDEN RETRIEVER

Playmate of adults and children, the Golden Retriever is a good, affectionate and very polite dog. Surely all these factors make it one of the most loved by families. He listens to his owners and if he is rebuked, he humbly returns with his tail between his legs aware that he has done some error. It is a breed that adapts very much to the situation and environment in which it lives.

5. AUSTRALIAN SHEPHERD

The Australian Shepherd can learn everything and well in no time. He is brave, curious, hyperactive (but gracefully), eager to fulfill the wishes and wishes of his family members, so much so that he would go along his owner to every world angle! These qualities have made it an excellent shepherd dog and a suitable four-legged dog for people search and rescue.

Not only that, always remind that the training given to a puppy is fundamental to teach him to behave in the right way even when there are humans around him.

Special considerations for guard and defense dogs

Although they look the same, guard dogs and guard dogs are two very different genres. Yes, their job could suggest the same type of activity (or rather, defense), but in reality, we are talking about two rather different types. Yes, because although many claim to have both defense and guard dogs, the reality is absolutely different: one cannot be good guard dogs, and excellent defense dogs. Let's see the difference together.

In reality, to have a good defense dog, a simple training is enough that anyone can get their 4-legged friend to do. Training, in fact, provides for the dog to be placed close to the owner: at this point, the trainer will cause him some minor annoyance to make him understand that when he growls showing annoyance, the trainer will stop harassing him by moving away. Obviously, the usual tasty morsels are useful to reward the dog.

In a short time, and by following this simple training, your dog will be able to understand when he should growl and when (even) he should bite. In this way it will become an excellent defense dog. On the other hand, the situation for the guard dog is different: his training is different, and the right qualities are needed. First of all, it's important to understand that a good watchdog will be especially effective when its owners are not present in the house. Precisely for this reason it would be better to use a pair of guard dogs. Furthermore, the decisions will not be imposed by a trainer, but will be made by the animal.

The latter will not have rewards, after having done his job, nor pampering or special attention. The watchdog, in fact, will have only one merit: the satisfaction of seeing the stranger flee from his own territory. Having defended the home of one's masters is, without a doubt, the greatest gratitude.

The main characteristic of a guard dog is independence: the animal, in fact, must not be distracted by any kind of weakness, be it a treat or a caress. This type of attitude is very important and clearly denotes the distinction between defense dog and guard dog. In fact, the former has been trained since he was a child, but he sees it all as a game.

The guard dog, on the other hand, is trained not to get distracted. Furthermore, his decision-making power is really high (let's remember that we are talking about an animal, and not a person): his instinct will lead him towards strangers, and his head will tell him how to behave.

Ultimately, a guard dog (after the most appropriate training) must absolutely possess the ability to act independently and without the presence of the master. This is a typical attitude, and verifiable, in sheep guard dogs. On the contrary, the personal defense dog is suitable for managing the management of animals, thanks to the innate predisposition to carry out orders given by its master.

Special considerations for working dogs

Working dogs are animals selected and trained to perform specific tasks in the service of man. Thanks to their intelligence, learning ability and physical resistance, working dogs are used in various sectors, including agriculture, police, civil protection and rescue.

What are the most common working dog breeds and what are they used for?

There are numerous working dog breeds, selected for their physical and behavioral characteristics. Among the most common breeds we find:

- ✓ German shepherd: used above all in the military and police fields.
- ✓ Doberman: employed in private security and civil protection.
- ✓ Rottweiler: mainly used as a guard dog.
- ✓ Labrador retriever: used in the rescue and assistance of disabled people.
- ✓ Golden retriever: mainly used as a guide dog for the blind.

A working dog should possess some key characteristics, including:

- ✓ Intelligence and learning ability.
- ✓ Physical endurance and resistance to stress.
- ✓ Instinct of protection and defense.
- ✓ Reliability and obedience to the master.

✓ Adaptability to different situations and environments.

To speak instead of the differences between a working dog and a companion dog, a working dog is selected and trained to perform specific tasks, while a companion dog is intended to live predominantly in the family as a pet. Working dogs therefore have a stronger and more determined character, while pet dogs are generally more sociable and affectionate.

In an urban environment, a working dog can be employed in a variety of tasks, including:

✓ Guard and protection of public and private buildings.
✓ Search for missing or missing persons.
✓ Interventions in case of emergencies, such as earthquakes or floods.
✓ Assistance to people with disabilities, for example as a guide dog or deaf-mute dog.
✓ Escort and support to the police forces during land control operations and investigations.

Training techniques for working dogs must be specific and targeted according to the task that the dog will have to perform. Among the most used techniques we find:

✓ Positive training, which involves the use of rewards and rewards to encourage the dog to follow a command.
✓ Clicker training, a technique that uses an audible clicker to tell the dog when it has performed a command correctly.
✓ Target training, which involves training the dog to follow a specific object or cue to perform an action.
✓ Negative reinforcement training, which involves using pressure or a cue to let your dog know that he needs to stop an unwanted behavior.

Special considerations for toy breeds

Let's make a small premise here: a small dog of a toy breed has the same needs as a large dog simply because a dog is a dog regardless of size.

So why offer an education course specifically designed for toy breeds?

Because it often happens that people, whether family or strangers, approach a small dog in a different way, unknowingly favoring the development of various problems that undermine the well-being of the dog and peaceful coexistence.

So when it comes to training a large breed dog or a small breed dog, the difference is not only in their abilities but also in the needs of their humans. A large dog must learn to respond to the "stay" command in any situation and to "party" in a more delicate way. Large dogs must receive effective training and be more docile than small dogs so that they can coexist with humans in complete safety.

The differences between training large dogs and training small dogs are almost imperceptible. In fact, virtually the same commands, positive reinforcement methods, and techniques are used to train dogs of any size.

Sometimes, however, these small differences could cause the training of a 4-legged friend not to have the desired success. Below you will find some useful advice on the best training techniques for toy breed dogs.

✓ For a small dog, you are huge. Unfortunately, one of the mistakes that owners of small dogs often make is to "overpower" their 4 legs, which could therefore get scared. The word "overstay" means standing leaning forward towards a small dog: in fact, the 4-legged could interpret this movement as a threat. This could make him nervous and therefore prevent him from learning adequately. So, how to train a small dog the right way? Here's the answer: instead of leaning forward, assume an upright posture or kneel and remember to make everything in front of and not above the dog.

✓ Getting in the right position is important. You've started sitting or kneeling in front of your small dog during training sessions. Everything is going great, but if you assume a different position when you give your 4-legged the commands "sit" or "down", he looks at you as if you were completely crazy. The problem is that your dog just can't generalize. Think that "sit" means that he should sit only when you are also sitting. He doesn't understand that this command only applies to his position, not yours. There is a solution: as soon as your dog learns to recognize the command while you are sitting, he tries to give him the same command, but changing your position a bit. For example, you might get down on your knees, somewhere between sitting and standing. When your dog begins to recognize the command even if you are not sitting, he continues the training by standing up more and more, for example by standing up with your knees bent, until you assume a fully upright position.

✓ A small dog has a small stomach. Food isn't the only reward when trying to train a dog, but it's definitely the easiest reward to use. Unfortunately, however, small-breed dogs fill up quickly and may find it more difficult to digest very substantial and fatty foods. If a dog feels full or has a tummy ache, he certainly won't be motivated by treats during training. If you use food as a reward, remember that your dog should only receive a very small amount. A crumb-sized piece of chicken or turkey is more than enough for a small dog. You can try to give him a little baby food with your finger too. Cheese and fatty foods like beef or pork aren't bad for large dogs, but they often cause digestive problems in small dogs, so you'll want to choose leaner foods.

✓ Some positions are more difficult for small dogs. As we said above every dog is unique and one should never generalize when it comes to canine skills. However, according to trainers, in most cases, small dogs have more difficulty than large dogs in learning the "sit" or "down" commands.

If your dog cannot learn these commands, it will take some time, patience and persistence on your part. For example, breaking the larger movement into small, simple movements is key.

Instead of trying to get your dog to lie down right away, follow these steps:

1. Reward your dog if he lowers his head and looks at the ground.

2. Encourage him to stretch out one of his front legs and reward him when he does.

3. Continue with these small steps until he is completely flat on the ground.

4. Otherwise, an alternative is to "condition" your dog's behavior. Keep an eye on him and pay attention to when he sits or lies down spontaneously. The moment he takes this action, show him that you are happy and reward him with something incredible.

5. The more dogs are rewarded for spontaneous behavior, the more they tend to repeat it. When you notice that, in your presence, your dog sits all the time, you can start giving this position a name, for example "sit". Say the command just when your 4-legged begins to sit up.

6. With a little practice, your dog will be able to associate the voice command with the action and will learn to act correctly when you say "sit" or "down".

Tips for addressing breed-specific behavior traits

Finally, here you are some general considerations for addressing dog breed specific behavior traits.

There are more than four hundred dog breeds, which differ greatly in physical appearance and behavior.

When discussing the behavioral differences between dog breeds it is helpful to distinguish between breed specific behavior patterns and more general breed differences in personality or temperament. In fact, there are typical characteristics that define some dog breeds such as the love of water of the Retriever, the "steadiness" of the Pointer or the tendency of the Border Collie to be attracted by things that move. However, differences in personality traits are considered aspects of the general character or behavioral "style" of each dog breed and are often referenced in the breed's standards. The Kennel Clubs underline the behavioral characteristics of each breed of dog through information campaigns and by alerting aspiring owners of the dog's working origins and of the problems that could arise with a family that is poorly suited to its needs. the Border Collie, for example, is a dog breed described as "a sharp-tempered, alert, responsive and intelligent dog. Not nervous or aggressive, but needs plenty of exercise, loves company and takes an enthusiastic part in any activity. Dedicated to the service of man but endowed with an extreme need to work to be happy, so much so that he suffers if forced all day in the kennel next to the hearth".

While for the Beagle one of the descriptions can be "there is no more pleasant sight than a pack of Beagles intent on hunting, their faces bent to sniff the ground, their tails straight and tidy, concentrated on the chase. The natural predatory instinct of this dog is also manifested in daily activities, such as a walk in the park: the man with a leash in his hand and no dog nearby is undoubtedly the owner of a Beagle". in terms of trainability and speed of learning the instructions given by the owner, in general, sporting and working breeds of dogs (English Springer Spaniel, Golden Retriever, Labrador Retriever, Poodle, Rottweiler and Border Collie) tended to obtain high scores for this aspect, while Hounds (Basset hound), Dachshunds, Terriers (West Highland White Terrier and Yorkshire Terrier) and Siberian Husky obtained low scores but, within the same breed. The differences between working and show lines were even more marked than the differences between different breeds. In any case, whether it's a Dachshund, a Dalmatian, a German Shepherd, we know that every breed has its own characteristics and peculiarities, not just aesthetics. It is precisely this that makes living together with each furry a unique and always different experience, but on the other hand it also imposes the need to calibrate the educational methodology based on the temperament of the individual dog.

Now let's briefly see some tips for behavioral training based on the various breeds.

Shepherd dogs

Sheepdogs are intelligent, territorial and obedient, of course when trained right.

Born as a working breed, these dogs feel accomplished in carrying out precise tasks.

Cattlemen

Dogs in the Cattle Dog category learn very quickly and need a lot of stimulation, both physically and mentally.

They are very independent and therefore need a very authoritative human point of reference.

Molossians

Dogs belonging to the Molossoid group have a very territorial nature and are always ready to defend their pack tooth and nail.

They need an authoritative and coherent education, but equally empathetic.

Getting two adult dogs of this species to get along can be quite a challenge, which certainly also complicates any joint training project.

The fact that giant-sized dogs are considered relatively late adults compared to other furry dogs plays in your favor: this means that you have a little more time to try to educate them.

Breeds: Bullmastiff, Great Dane.

These dogs bring together the characteristics of territoriality and independence of their cousins.

Cattle Dogs and Molossians

Their training requires a certain dog experience: certainly, they are not dogs always ready to obey any order, but it is true that consistent education from an authoritative point of reference can give excellent results. Not inclined to practice dog sports, they need a lot of outdoor space in which to give vent to their nature as shepherds.

Better to train them without the distraction of other specimens, even if socialization is very important for them.

Breeds: Kuvasz, Komondor.

Terrier

Terriers are what are commonly referred to as "hunting dogs".

Precisely because of the purpose for which they were originally bred, alongside virtues such as courage and independence these dogs can also show a rather aggressive attitude.

In training a Terrier, therefore, it is important to be careful not to positively reinforce behavior of this type. If, on the one hand, they are very independent, solitary and absolutely not very patient dogs, they are also very intelligent: with a little experience it will not be difficult to obtain a good level of education. A joint training is conceivable only with specimens with a good basic socialization.

Breeds: Jack Russell Terrier, Lakeland Terrier

Bull-type Terriers, the result of crossing bulldogs and terriers, were initially bred with the aim of helping butchers in killing bulls and later also used in bloody dog fights.

Despite the ominous past, they are extremely affectionate dogs and, if well educated, show a strong and self-confident character.

Breeds: American Pit Bull Terriers.

Dachshunds

Definitely intelligent and docile, characteristics that prove to be excellent allies during training, Dachshunds can also be nice big heads.

They certainly do not accept any order from above with resignation, but they always try to have their say. They are very courageous dogs and, like Terriers, not very sociable.

A good education, made up of coherence, gentleness and patience, can make the Dachshund an example of obedience.

Spitz

Spitz are very independent dogs, with a strong protective instinct and a guarding nature but absolutely disinterested in pleasing their human.

Asian Spitz are more prone to hunting than European specimens.

These dogs form an unbreakable bond with their human while being especially wary of both strangers and their own kind.

Breeds: German Spitz, Shiba Inu.

Among the breeds belonging to this group, the Japanese Spitz is the easiest to educate in fact, it differs greatly from its European relatives in character.

Greyhounds

Greyhounds are very autonomous dogs and love to go their own way. A nice run certainly satisfies them more than exercises and mental stimulation.

Short-haired greyhounds in particular develop a relationship of great affection with their humans.

They have a strong predatory instinct so be careful to let them run free in large, unfenced spaces. In this, the Irish Greyhound is an exception, not inclined to hunt but very cooperative with its human. Precisely because of this stubborn temperament it is better to reserve one-on-one training sessions for the Greyhounds.

Some final tip

Here you are some final tips to address your dog behavior:

✓ There are breeds that need dynamism, a life in the open air and frequent walks, others indicated if you live in more restricted environments. We must always consider the natural habitat from which a particular breed derives, forcing a husky to live in a small apartment in the city where high temperatures are reached in summer would not be a good choice for the furry friend.

✓ To best train and direct a dog's behavior it is necessary to get in tune with him, understand his language and allow him to understand us. In this regard it is useful to express what we want through the ways that he himself uses and therefore understands, i.e., through facial expressions, eyes, mouth, head, gestures and body position. It is also essential to use the correct tone of voice based on the command you want to give. A dirty look accompanied by a severe and decisive "no" will make him understand that he has done something wrong, while a "good" accompanied by a nice smile, a friendly voice and a pat on the side will convey consent. Care must be taken that facial language, tone of voice and gestures do not diverge since the animal, not understanding the words, understands a command, an appreciation or whatever from the combination of these three factors.

✓ The dog also expresses its emotions with the posture of the body, with the tail and the position of the paws, and obviously by barking and growling.

✓ Before starting training, it is important that the dog recognizes the hierarchical order within the family, by instinct it is in fact led to identify a pack leader, a sort of guide, a master to whom he will be submissive and obey. In this regard, dogs have, like people, preferences and the leader of the pack, the subject who imposes himself the most, does not always

60

coincide with his favorite; dominant dogs, for example, can enter in conflict in the face of an imposed authority, in which case the owner will have to be able to bring down that wall to establish a serene and peaceful coexistence. It should always be kept in mind, however, that the characteristics we are talking about cannot absolutely be valid for all dogs and must therefore be interpreted with flexibility.

✓ It doesn't matter whether you have a purebred or a mixed-breed furry by your side, what matters is getting to know him well in order to calibrate the educational methodology on his specific characteristics.

✓ Finally, don't overdo the training and remember that for specimens who are not used to living with other similar ones, the mere fact of sharing some exercises with another paw friend is already a great life lesson.

Ended this one, in the next chapter we will explain how to build a strong bond with your dog.

Chapter 3: Building a Strong Bond with Your Dog

Building a strong bond with your dog is an important part of dog ownership. This chapter covers the importance of positive reinforcement training, understanding your dog's body language and communication cues, and building trust and affection through training and play.

The importance of positive reinforcement training

Let's start by trying to understand what positive reinforcement is and the importance it has in building a bond with the adult dog. Positive reinforcement is a positive stimulus to demonstrate for a behavior that we want to maintain or reinforce.

Positive reinforcement is a technique that consists in rewarding with caresses, affectionate words, snacks or games when the dog obeys an order.

This process is undoubtedly more fun and enjoyable for both you and your furry friend. All dogs would rather receive a treat as a reward than be punished and tied to a chain.

Dogs learn by association (two associated events are perceived as cause and effect even when, in fact, they are not) and as also happens to humans, the more positive an association is, the more its memory puts chemical roots in the brain. But how do you make an association positive? To teach a dog a behavior, some educators today adopt the operant model. Simplifying: when the animal proposes a certain behavior during work sessions, it learns that some of its actions are rewarded, while others leave the handler indifferent. Translated into dog language, the right action turns into a cookie or a game. To formalize this relationship, already in the thirties of the last century, it was Burrhus F. Skinner, a behaviorist psychologist who had defined reinforcement as an action that increases the probability of seeing a behavior repeated: the cookie received as a reward, in exchange for a seated.

These positive sensations are ingested by our four-legged friend and direct him to behave in the same way (the correct one) as when he received the positive reinforcement for the first time. Therefore, gradually, the dog will gradually become more and more cooperative and willing to obey its owner.

Let's always remember that dogs are much smarter than some people think. Thanks to the positive reinforcement, they will feel safer and will perceive being with the owners as pleasant.

There is no dog that would rather be severely punished than be rewarded properly if he behaves right.

The important aspect in this learning methodology is that the positive reinforcement must be given immediately after a correct action and that the reward must be hidden before this behavior. Let's give an example: if your dog does his business outside the home correctly, you must immediately insert a positive reinforcement that was not there before. In case you enter it earlier or later, the dog will be confused and less willing to repeat the taste behavior.

The benefits of positive reinforcement are many, which is why it is recommended by trainers and veterinarians. Among other things, it allows you to strengthen the dog-master bond, makes the animal feel loved and respected and serves to resolve some past trauma.

It is very important to let your dog know that you are rewarding him for obeying commands.

It should be noted that every owner knows his own specimen, so it's up to us humans to know what will give him the most pleasure as a reward. There is therefore no universal rule about which tools to use as a reward. Some dogs prefer a reward that fills their stomach, so food will allow them to double their efforts in exercises, others will prefer to play or again, specimens are very tactile, they will be satisfied with a caress.

The downside of positive reinforcement is that you can't give him a treat or pet him if you don't give him an order he has to obey, because he won't understand why you're rewarding him.

Understanding your dog's body language and communication cues

The dog-owner relationship can be a wonderful thing, provided it is based on respect and real mutual knowledge.

Every owner will inevitably be a point of reference for a dog's life.

To establish a healthy and lasting relationship over time, it will first of all be essential to learn to understand his world, then it will be necessary to define the rules, finally it will be necessary to love each other.

The dog must be able to understand that he can trust his master, while the owner must learn to interpret his gestures, his requests and his needs, to become a good leader. In this paragraph we will talk about the relationship between dog and owner, and we will cover these topics:

✓ Rules for establishing the correct dog-owner relationship.

✓ When correct communication is a great gesture of love.

✓ Love is the right compromise.

63

So, communication is vital important and understand dogs body language could be the first step for this purpose. The dog, in fact, uses its own body to communicate intentions but also emotions.

Your dog then communicates to you all the time. If you understand what he's saying, you'll improve a deeper bond of trust and respect. But it could be also helpful in predicting his behavior and prevent problems.

Dog body language: position

The dog uses its body to communicate emotions and intentions. Sometimes, dog body language is simply unfamiliar, other times, it's at odds with what that same signal means to a human, such as yawning or looking away.

Wagging the tail

Tail wagging is one of the main body language signals in a dog. A wagging tail means the dog is emotionally excited. To interpret the dog's emotions and intentions, it is necessary to observe the speed and direction of wagging and the position of the tail. The faster the movement, the more excited the dog is. If you think about those long, slow side-to-side tails your dog makes when he greets you, that means the dog is relaxed!

Hairs straight

When the hair along a dog's back is raised it is a clear sign that the dog is excited, but not necessarily in a negative way. The dog could be upset or stressed, but he could also be excited or strongly interested in something. It is often and not voluntary reaction: think about goosebumps in people.

Posture

A dog's weight distribution can communicate a lot about his mood and intentions. For example, a dog curled up symbolizes that he is scared or stressed. On the other hand, when the dog rolls onto his back exposing his belly, it may appear that he requires a belly rub, or that he is relaxed, which is often the case but in reality, it can be a sign of considerable stress and anxiety.

When the dog positions himself with his weight shifted forward, he is trying to get closer to something indicating his interest. But it could also indicate offensive intentions.

A less easy to understand signal is the lifting of the paw. In hunting breeds such as the English Setter, the lifting of the paw is part of its hunting aptitude and indicates that the prey is near.

Facial expressions

Dogs have likable facial features to people, but they don't employ these expressions the same manner.

For example, many of us yawn when are tired or bored, but dogs yawn when they're stressed. Lip licking is another dog body language signal that people often misinterpret. A confusing facial expression is the smile. Normally, when dogs bare their teeth, its purpose is to warn.

Eyes

You can see many things about your dog's condition by looking at his eyes. For this purpose, a dog's eyes can be soft or hard. Soft eyes show relaxed lids and sometimes it seems that the dog is squinting, this indicates that he is calm or happy. Once they have hard eyes, this means a negative state of mind.

Dog body language and food

The dog also uses body movements to communicate that it is time for a meal. To get our attention he can come to us, bark or lick the bowl. These are all signs with which the dog tells us that he wants to eat. You can choose to give your dog personalized fresh food plans that arrive ready-made directly to your home, in this way you can feed your dog with fresh and natural meals tailor-made for him.

For your part however, learning to communicate with your dog is essential for a balanced and positive coexistence, as well as for improving your relationship with him by trying to understand what he wants to tell you at all times.

On several occasions, a lack of understanding between dog and man can be the cause of unwanted behavior, precisely due to non-verbal bad communication.

The greatest gesture of love that an owner can do to his dog is to communicate correctly towards him.

Here are some tips on how to best relate to your dog:

✓ Always employ a high-pitched tone and a low tone of voice so that the dog does not confuse your words with a punishment. Also, you must remember that he has very sensitive hearing, so you don't need to raise your voice to make yourself heard.

✓ Try to combine words with gestures: in this way the dog will understand you better and it will be easier for him to understand you in noisy places.

✓ Use positive reinforcement, such as a snack to communicate with the dog; various studies show that these animals learn better with this technique than with punishment.

- ✓ Make eye contact with the dog when communicating with him.
- ✓ Always respect the dog, especially if you see that he doesn't feel comfortable.
- ✓ If the dog doesn't understand you, repeat the action but never scold him.

Building trust and affection through training and play

Our book on how to educate an adult dog end with a reflection on bond building, which is particularly important. In fact, remember that your dog may have been left in a kennel, or raised without too much attention from previous owners. If possible, try to find out more about her past to get the full picture. He may be afraid of something in particular or may have developed a trust issue that you should be aware of.

Welcome your new friend with open arms and make sure you have plenty of time to play, feel good together, take care of him and get some exercise. In fact, the game strengthens the bond between dog and owner, improves well-being, stimulates attention and respond positively to training amd physical exercise. This will be very useful on strengthening your bond and make your dog more incline to do these activities. The game is therefore a fundamental component of the relationship between dog and owner, as it helps to strengthen the bond with our four-legged friend.

Not only that, but the game also contributes to improving the well-being of the dog and, why not, that of the owner. It also stimulates attention, exercise and fun. Playing with your dog, therefore, does not simply mean carrying out a playful activity, but also implementing actions to the benefit of the physical and mental health of the four-legged. In this case, the classic "pull the ball!", the "pull and drop" or even going for a run or an energetic fight attract the dog's attention which is directed only to its own human, the only one it interacts with during playful activity. Without a doubt, when dogs and their owners exercise and play together, their emotional bond is strengthened. Since exercise is a stimulating activity, sharing it creates a positive strengthening of the friendship, as well as increasing the dog's trust in us.

Finally, reward him regularly when he does what you ask, such as crouching down in moments of relaxation, responding to calls or walking on a leash in an orderly manner.

PART 3: MENTAL EXERCISE FOR DOGS

Introduction

After talking about the "physical" training of puppies and adult dogs, the time has come, in this third guide, to also talk about the dog's mental health. There will be in fact examined all the proper mental exercise for dogs. All the benefits we will underline and the importance of regular mental exercise for a dog's overall health

Chapter 1: Mental Exercise for Dogs

Dogs need both physical and mental exercise to stay healthy and happy. This chapter covers the benefits of mental stimulation for dogs and includes training exercises that challenge the mind (such as scent work, puzzle toys). It also covers the importance of regular mental exercise for a dog's overall health.

The benefits of mental stimulation for dogs

Dog mental activation is a wonderful methodology that all pet or working dog owners can apply with incredible benefits. The dog is an intelligent animal, even if we often underestimate its capabilities. In fact, very often we worry about providing adequate physical activity, but then we forget to train his mind, as well as his body. When we approach mental activation, however, we realize that our four-legged friend has many abilities, but also needs to use his brain.

So, one thing is certain: dogs have minds and even if we take them for walks, we make them run with other dogs, we make them play with the ball or the tug of war, we rarely offer them the opportunity to use their cognitive abilities and even more rarely we know how to stimulate their mind. Instead, it is very important to stimulate our dogs and offer them intelligent activities.

In fact, our dog's mental health is essential: it is not only necessary to train his agility, enhance his physical abilities, but also to try in every way to increase his general mental well-being. It is in fact very important that the owner of a dog does everything to allow the psychological well-being of the animal to which he requires to live by his side (and not just worrying when he gets sick).

Mental activation games for dogs are playful activities that stimulate his intelligence and cognitive ability. This type of game consists of placing the dog in front of a problem whose solution will earn him a reward. This type of mental activation has several benefits as in this way the dog will have to focus on finding the solution and, in case of success, in addition to the reward, his self-esteem will greatly benefit. Mind activating games can be bought for a few dollars, so they are very cheap, alternatively, with a little imagination and creativity they can also be made at home.

A high benefit concerns the fact that Mental Activation can be used by everyone, since it does not require any previous training. In Mental Activation the dog learns by attempts that he proposes spontaneously and learns to emit more frequently those behaviors that lead him to success, expanding his heuristics.

The only thing that is needed to start, for any type of dog, is the motivation, the desire to reach that coveted prize. For this reason, the handler must carefully choose something that the dog likes very much, which stimulates him to work hard to face and solve the puzzle.

Another benefit, in addition to the increase in your dog's self-esteem, is linked to the fact that continuous and functional mental stimulation is the best solution to avoid behavioral problems: an insecure dog, in fact, is much more prone to aggression. Mental stimulation also has a tiring and at the same time calming effect: this is why it is essential to satisfy its real needs.

According to various authors, among which we point out Dr. Joel Dehasse, Veterinary Behaviorist, mental activity is 10 times more tiring than physical activity.

But there is one important thing to underline at this point: mental activity does get tiring, but it does it in a different way than physical activity. To be more specific, the effect of a sniffing or mental activation game is to tire in a positive way, leaving the dog calmer and ready to rest. After physical activity, however, the dog remains excited and does not rest, just like we do. And a relaxed dog and a happier dog! But think about it better: to have a happier dog, consequently, aren't we happier too? And there is no greater benefit than this.

To summarize everything, we have said so far, Mental Activation brings numerous benefits to the dog and to our relationship with him. The apartment animal will find a way to engage the mind and focus on cognitive activities that will tire it in a healthy way, it will have the opportunity to "earn its bread" (the prize) by implementing and perfecting its strategies and skills by nature. Among other benefits we have:

✓ The dog will have interesting and stimulating activities to devote himself to and for which to use energy, rather than venting it in unwanted behaviors.

✓ The dog learns to use different skills according to the problems he has to solve and will be able to transfer the acquired skills to new problems similar to the previous ones. By facing increasingly difficult problems and discovering that he is able to solve them, the dog learns to live difficult situations better and therefore to manage stress in a positive way.

✓ At the same time, he will gain more self-confidence.

✓ It will be possible for a dog to better develop its cognitive abilities, learn to relate proactively with unknown objects rather than fearing them, develop better concentration skills and to

70

tolerate stress; he will be able to regain confidence in his own abilities, reactivate and recover self-esteem and therefore serenity.

✓ It allows the dog to acquire new skills, to implement and perfect strategies and skills with which he is naturally gifted.

✓ Stimulate and improve the dog's cognitive ability.

✓ Tired in a positive way (it is 10 times more tiring than physical activity, and relaxes the dog, tiring him in a healthy way)

✓ Getting the dog used to face problems with less stress and frustration. By facing increasingly difficult problems and discovering that he is able to solve them, the dog learns to live difficult situations better and therefore to manage stress in a positive way.

✓ It allows the dog to purposefully relate to unknown objects instead of fearing them.

✓ Develop more effective ways of thinking in the dog.

✓ Increase your fitness, i.e., your ability to adapt and cope with new situations.

✓ Increase your self-esteem, self-confidence and self-confidence.

✓ Stimulate the most apathetic or elderly subjects.

✓ It can be used for dogs with control and self-control difficulties, for hyperactive subjects who need to learn to calm down and reflect.

Training exercises that challenge the mind (e.g., scent work, puzzle toys, etc.)

Mental activation exercises are essentially games that involve and test the dog's intelligence and represent a fun and intelligent method to educate them. In other words, are exercises that challenge our dog's mind. Usually, they consist of putting the dog in front of a problem whose solution will lead him to earn a reward. Furthermore, they can also serve as pastimes for lonely dogs, who spend many hours at home without the owner's company. In short, they are a guaranteed boredom chaser, an excellent way to keep the dog busy at home without him attacking furniture, cushions and various objects and to get him used to behaving in the best way.

But what are the games that stimulate your dog's mental activation?

There are all types on the market, and they are different in type of activity, level of difficulty and size. As we shall see, some are real brain teasers! You don't need to go shopping at the pet store to stimulate a dog's brain though. There are mind games that require nothing more than your participation and some kibble as positive reinforcement.

Let's find out which exercises and devises are most suitable for stimulating the intelligence and cognitive abilities of our four-legged friend.

The Kong

The Kong is a rigid container where you can insert food that our dog likes inside. The aim of the game is to make sure that the dog understands how to get the food out of the object. This game is very suitable for anxious dogs and those who suffer from fear of abandonment. The effort to understand how the Kong works stimulates intelligence and increases concentration with enormous benefits for the health of our puppy.

Masticators or chewers

By chew we mean a container inside which you will have to put a small amount of food as a reward, which the dog will have to try to pull out with his teeth, mouth, tongue and paws. This type of game is very suitable for dogs suffering from separation anxiety, as it keeps them engaged and stimulated, and at the same time they manage to vent their tension. There are also real dental snacks that have the same entertainment purpose but at the same time take care of the dog's oral hygiene. Furthermore, thanks to its serrated shape, it is capable of cleaning your dog's teeth quickly and easily. However, please always supervise your dog while he enjoys nibbling him!

Interactive tables

There are various types of interactive tables on the market, from tik-tok to tris. The first consists of a table with several compartments in which to hide a treat, and the dog will have to try to figure out how to open the flap and get his reward. It is a game that allows you to develop your sense of smell and perspicacity. Tris, on the other hand, is the classic game in which your dog will have to choose which container the crunchy is hidden under. Thanks to the table, your supervision is not necessary, but in case you want to play with him you can simply do it even with paper cups.

Cube ball

In this game the reward is not the food, but the ball contained inside a cube. The game consists in letting the dog find a way to get the ball out of the cube.

This game works like that of the Kong, but instead of containing food, a ball is stuck inside it which the dog must try to get out. It's the perfect toy for dogs that don't move much and can't go overboard with snacks between meals.

Puzzle tous

If your dog has an innate hunting instinct but no way to vent it, this game is for him. These are simple puppets or objects that emit sounds or even simulate the movements of small animals such as birds, rodents, etc. and that bear their likenesses. It is not a real mental exercise, but it allows you to keep your four-legged active and free to express its nature. Pay close attention to the materials with which they are made and make sure they are not toxic or made up of small ingestible parts. Your dog's health is worth more than anything!

The tick tock

The tic tac is made up of four containers closed by flaps. The game consists in hiding a morsel of food inside one of the containers and waiting for the dog to study the way to find it. To find his favorite food, the dog will have to learn to open the doors. Sometimes the dog may not immediately understand how the game works. If he finds the tidbit right away, he could continue to look for it under the other doors too, or if he doesn't find it, he could be upset and disappointed. As with any new business, you need to give your friend time to learn and gain experience.

Look for hidden objects: the scent work

This game can be played at home at any time. The game consists in hiding morsels of food or toys in some secret places in the house. The dog will have to find the treasure by following his instincts and smells. Hidden object hunting is a simple activity to organize but at the same time it is very stimulating for the dog.

Educational games for dogs to play together

These games are to be considered a training to improve your dog's obedience. Remember, you should do them together with your furry friend for no more than 15 minutes to avoid stressing him out.

Get on and off

This is a useful exercise to make your dog concentrate on his body and the space around him. If you have a garden all the better, but unless you have a Great Dane you can also do this exercise indoors with solid and stable stools or chests. Here's what you need to do: snacks in the closed hand and commands away. The first few times it will be important to accompany the word with the movement of the body.

Guessing the hand

It's a very simple way to make your dog's brain more stimulated; You can only employ some snacks. The game consists of taking some snacks in one of your hands and letting the dog guess which one they are in. Easy and fast.

Guessing the Cup

It's another very easy to do mind game for dogs. Three cups are used: you have to hide a snack under one of them (while the animal is watching) and then mix. This game will give your pet an opportunity to practice their problem-solving skills.

Here the paw

An evergreen that always comes in handy for teaching your dog to respond to your commands. Your role will consist of holding a treat with a clenched fist and only opening it when your dog responds to the command to give you a paw. Don't worry if at first your dog will react in totally different ways than he should, with time and patience he will learn.

Obstacle course

Obstacle courses are a hybrid between physical activity and intelligence games for dogs, as the body and mind are involved in a dual effort at the same time. For your pet they are a real hoot, and to create a path you will only need commonly used objects such as boxes, cushions, broomsticks, books, etc. Follow the path forward with a snack in your hand.

Simple rules to follow in mind activation games for dogs

How to choose the right game to stimulate his intelligence?

Intelligence games are not all the same and the choice at first glance may not seem so simple. First, make sure that the toy is safe, i.e., made of non-toxic materials or with detachable or sharp parts that can hurt your dog. This also applies to homemade dog toys, DIY is ok, but the watchword must be safety.

Before starting, it is of course necessary to know the rules, which in the case of Mental Activation are few, simple and mainly dictated by common sense. They are some simple rules to follow to make mental activation games for dogs effective:

- ✓ Simplicity.
- ✓ Do not incite. the dog must not be encouraged to play a game, the owner proposes it without saying or doing anything.
- ✓ Graduality. it is important to propose games that the dog can solve, starting with the simple ones and progressing following the dog's answers.
- ✓ Does not continue until a drawer has been closed. Only when the dog has solved a game, can you continue with a more difficult one.
- ✓ Do not help. If the dog seems distressed or is asking for help, the owner should ignore it. at most he can increase motivation by moving the game or adding more food.
- ✓ 20 minutes max. Sessions should not last longer than twenty minutes.
- ✓ Knowing how to take a step back. If the dog hasn't been able to solve a game within 20 minutes, then we will propose a simpler game.
- ✓ End with a success. Sessions must always end in success.
- ✓ Do not reward. when the dog succeeds in solving a game, the owner should not reward it with praise or pats.
- ✓ Freedom of action. The dog must be able to do whatever he wants and deems appropriate to solve the problem, without the owner intervening or interrupting him. this is why it is important to offer safe games in an appropriate environment.
- ✓ Always supervise. Mental activation must always and only be done under the supervision of the owner, never leave the dog alone with problem solving games.

With a little imagination and effort you can create fun games that are useful and stimulating for our four-legged friend at the same time.

The importance of regular mental exercise for a dog's overall health

As we have seen in general, recurring mental stimulation is important because it gives pets the opportunity to exercise their bodies and, at the same time, explore their surroundings and learn new skills. There are so many ways to interact with your dog that aren't just about walking and cuddling together. It is very important to be able to let the dog vent with activities that also engage his mind and not just through physical activity, so that he will always be responsive to your commands and requests. Every dog needs a fair amount of physical and mental activity. If we know how to provide it to him, we will make him a healthy, balanced and serene dog. However, physical activity alone is not enough, indeed, on the contrary, excess physical effort stresses the dog, obtaining just the opposite effect. The importance of continuous and regular mental exercise for dog concerns above all the ability of "Problem Solving". We know that this term indicates "the set of processes for analyzing, facing and positively solving problematic situations", and this is the purpose of Mental Activation games, in which a problem is proposed to the dog and the task of finding it is left to him. the way to solve it. Usually, as we have seen, food is hidden inside particular objects, and to reach the prize the dog must overcome difficulties that can vary greatly, such as moving an object, opening, lifting, pressing, turning, and so on. Depending on the type of problem proposed, the dog will have one or more methods to achieve the goal, and will have to reason, reflect, try and ingenuity by offering and experimenting with different behaviors to find the one suitable for solving the problem. A dog more inclined to problem solving is above all a dog very inclined to training and listening to our commands. But if there is something even more important, it is that mental regulation in dogs causes positive physiological and behavioral reactions, which are able, to a certain extent, to improve the quality of their life.

Mental stimulation in dogs induced through play, for example, generates a wide range of positive emotions. Some scientific reports state that, when played regularly and in a rewarding environment, it can trigger a variety of responses in the central nervous system.

In turn, these stimuli cause physiological and behavioral reactions rich in benefits for the animal. In the following lines we will talk about how play activities cause this mental stimulation in dogs. In fact, we must not forget that, after all, these are animals endowed with instincts that they must satisfy. Nowadays, it is a universally accepted fact that animals feel pain and are capable of suffering. We also understand that "animal welfare" is not only the absence of pain and fear, but also involves the presence of a stimulating environment.

It is important to remember that pleasure is usually evaluated in the context of temporary sensory stimulation, such as that related to the sense of taste.

Undoubtedly, it is difficult to measure the degree of well-being of an animal. Such situations include:

✓ The anticipation of positive rewards.

✓ The opportunities offered to animals to gather information, such as in the case of problem-solving experiences.

✓ Positive emotional experiences that persist over time or that are repeated regularly.

Let's not forget our bond with the dog: these regular exercises strengthen the relationship between us and the pet and stimulate the animal on a cognitive level.

In general, these processes aim to enhance long-term emotional states and keep good cognitive functioning in the dogs. This line of thought even manifests aspects of scientific interest, since also deepening the knowledge of the physiological mechanisms underlying the process of mental stimulation in dogs represents a fascinating activity.

There is one last thing to underline, before closing this third book: this type of activity can be practiced by any type of dog, but it shouldn't be a replacement for daily outings.

With this we have also finished all the explanations of our third book which has concerned the stimulation and mental well-being of our beloved dog. The next guide will focus instead on the appropriate nutrition of our dog.

PART 4: HOMEMADE DOG FOOD

Introduction

This guide number 4 will be completely dedicated to the nutrition of our 4-legged friend.

From the general guidelines, up to the recipes to feed our dog in the best possible way, you will find all possible information on its correct and functional nutrition. But what we would like to emphasize more is the importance of home-made nutrition, complete with controlled and specific food for our faithful friend.

Chapter 1: Homemade Dog Food

Feeding your dog, a healthy diet is important for their overall health and well-being. This chapter covers the benefits of feeding your dog a homemade diet, nutritional requirements for dogs, and includes recipes and guidelines for preparing balanced, healthy meals for your dog.

The benefits of feeding your dog a homemade diet

The term "domestic, or home, dog food" includes a heterogeneous set of nutritional methods ranging from the exclusive use of table scraps, up to the use of finely elaborated rations to satisfy the dog's nutritional needs. In the way it is classically conceived, the home ration is composed of a "meat-rice-carrot" mixture, enriched with a drizzle of oil, occasionally with a yolk, and sometimes with a specific vitamin-mineral complement. We therefore speak of a homemade diet for dogs when it is decided to replace processed food (industrial production) with human-grade food prepared at home. The various ingredients can naturally replace each other, since their nutritional value is roughly equivalent. However, in order not to make mistakes, it is important to know well which foods are allowed and which ones to avoid, or to be administered sparingly.

Attention! Homemade diet does not mean using the leftovers of what the dog's owner eats but buying and then cooking foods suitable for his needs. In the home diet, unprocessed and correctly balanced raw materials are used.

The benefits of the homemade diet, compared to that made up entirely of industrial feed, are numerous. To name a few of the most important:

✓ Lower presence of complex carbohydrates (cereal flours and starches) and therefore of sugars, energy currency of cancer cells.

✓ Sometimes when you change something, you don't see a big impact right away. When you feed your dog fresh food, the changes may not be visible immediately, but the science is clear: Over time, the benefits associated with a fresh diet can make your dog healthier and increase the time they spend together. Here are some of the long-term benefits of feeding human-grade ingredients, portioned with precision.

- ✓ Easy weight management, inflammation reduction and joint strengthening. Pre-portioned packs make weight management easier. Keeping your dog at the right weight can help prevent a number of diseases, including arthritis. Studies show that even a small reduction in weight can alleviate this painful condition. The fresh recipes that we will discuss in the third chapter also contain healthy Omega-3 fatty acids, which are able to reduce inflammation and improve arthritis.
- ✓ A stronger and healthier heart. Fresh, human-grade protein not only tastes really good for your dog, but it's also good for his heart.
- ✓ Increased protein intake: more and better-quality proteins for a healthier immune system.
- ✓ High digestibility and better assimilation of nutrients thanks to the presence of fibers and unsaturated fatty acids such as Omega-3.
- ✓ Improvement of the dog's mood. High-quality, fresh protein does more than just safeguard your dog's heart health. Research has shown that fresh food is easily digested and provides nutrients that can affect mood-related hormones such as serotonin. That means a happier dog.
- ✓ Less development of food allergies and intolerances related to the stages of intestinal inflammation and the accumulation of biogenic amines such as histamine (residues of sugar metabolism).
- ✓ Active presence of vitamins and antioxidants such as polyphenols or sulforaphanes present in fruit and vegetables (broccoli, cranberries, strawberries, etc.).
- ✓ Reducing the risk of obesity.
- ✓ Another of the reasons that commonly push owners towards this transition in their puppy's diet is the desire to provide him with more energy, a shinier and healthier coat, healthier teeth and decrease the problem of bad breath.

In short, we can say that home-made food is the best choice to ensure the long-term well-being of our four-legged friends. But, speaking of cons, one of the biggest disadvantages of the homemade diet is the large amount of time it takes to prepare. In fact, when we think about the preparation of the home diet, we must not limit ourselves to thinking about the cooking time of the food for our dog. In fact, one of the steps that requires the most time is to balance and dose all the ingredients which will then be placed in a bag or containers that allow for correct conservation.

It is always a better choice to trust on experienced veterinarians when it comes to feeding your dog properly. If, for example, the ingredients are not weighed and balanced correctly, the home-cooked diet could cause your dog more harm than good.

What distinguishes the homemade diet from other types of nutrition?

The homemade diet differs from other types of dog food in many ways. One of the most interesting and most innovative compared to other dog foods on the market is the ability to see the ingredients in the bowl. In fact, undergoing minimal processing, the ingredients can be distinguished with the naked eye, when in industrial food, the food is presented in the form of dry croquettes or gelatinous pate.

The real uniqueness of the homemade diet is that the ingredients will therefore be clearly visible and - if cooked in the right world - they will not need additives. Through adequate cooking, the nutrients will remain unchanged.

One of the differences that can be noticed more than others is how the dog, passing from industrial to home-made food, tends to drink less. This may be cause for concern at first, but it is completely normal. The 60% humidity present in the food of the home diet, compared to dry food, allows the dog to hydrate also thanks to the liquids present in the meal. For this reason, a dog fed a homemade diet needs to drink less frequently.

In industrial food, according to the labels, the sources of protein are much lower in number than in the home-made diet. On some industrial food labels, for example, you can read: 4% fresh chicken, while in the home-made diet, fresh protein sources reach up to 60%.

Home-made food, mainly made up of cooked and top-quality ingredients, should be kept in the fridge or freezer to keep it longer. Industrial food, on the other hand, has much longer deadlines and can be stored in cool places outside the refrigerator for months, consequently it also needs to be composed of preservatives.

The most substantial difference of the homemade diet compared to other types of food is the fact that it is much healthier for your dog, and this will allow him or her to have healthier meals and fewer allergies, and you to make fewer trips to the vet.

Nutritional requirements for dogs

To talk about our dog's nutritional requirements, we must start from a relatively simple question: how much food does my dog need?

81

There is no general answer that fits everyone, because a dog's nutritional needs depend on many factors. Here are the parameters you need to keep in mind, as a first step:

- ✓ The age of the dog
- ✓ The breed
- ✓ The weight in kg
- ✓ Activity level (are you very active or are you lazy? Are you pregnant? Are you breastfeeding?).

For a healthy diet suitable for the age of the dog, it is not only the vitamin and mineral content that counts: the right ration is the one that balances the energy value and proteins.

In this case, based on the weight of the dog, you can easily calculate the correct amount of food. If, on the other hand, you prefer to feed your pet by choosing the raw materials yourself, to adjust yourself you need to know some formulas to understand how much a dog should eat.

To calculate specifically the right amount of food for an adult dog, know that adult dogs no longer have to grow but at the same time have a higher energy expenditure than elderly dogs. So, what is the energy requirement of an adult dog?

Let's start at the base. Energy is expressed in megajoules (mj) or kilocalories (kcal). Using the Meyer and Zentek formula, you can easily calculate the average amount of energy your adult dog needs each day.

The energy requirement of adult dogs is equivalent to 124.2 kcal x kg0.75 of body weight.

For example: if your adult dog weighs 20 kg, his energy requirement will be equal to: 124.2 kcal x 20 kg0.75 = 1172.73 kcal per day.

As far as the protein requirement of the adult dog is concerned, we have already said that proteins are a fundamental component when it comes to dog nutrition. That said, you can use this formula to calculate the protein requirement of an adult dog: approximately 5 g of crude protein x 0.75 kg of body weight.

As for the other nutrients we have:

carbohydrates. Carbohydrate intake is important both as a rapidly available source of energy and as a regulator of bacterial flora activity. No problem for the assimilation of glucose and sucrose, but the dog often has difficulty digesting lactose.

- fats, but in the right measure. In his diet the fats must not exceed 10%; excesses not only lead to obesity, but also to an animal more predisposed to diseases (metabolic and cardio-vascular) and premature aging.

- vitamins, especially as a puppy and during pregnancy and breastfeeding. The dog is unable to synthesize all the vitamins, so some must be taken with the diet; specific vitamin deficiencies can lead to disease.

- minerals, which are present in different quantities in all foods. It is necessary to administer the right quantities with the diet, especially in puppies and pregnant dogs.

As it is possible to see from the formulas and indications given, it is difficult to be sure that you have not made errors in the calculations: for this reason, our advice is always to consult a veterinary surgeon who can check the correct intake of nutrients in the diet and possibly correct it. In this manner it will be possible for you to establish a correct homemade diet for your dog.

Guidelines for preparing balanced, healthy meals for your dog

The first thing we should worry about to understand if our dog's diet is healthy is to try to understand if the origin of the foods is natural or if they are highly processed ingredients. Often, the food we give to our dogs is full of preservatives, in fact the bags of food can stay on the supermarket shelves for months and months.

Another important factor to take into account to recognize if our dog's diet is healthy is the amount of food, we give him. In a healthy dog feeding program, each dog should receive a specific amount of food based on his needs.

Very often, however, the food they are given is leftovers from their owners' plates, or croquettes or industrial wet food, which is rarely weighed and portioned correctly. The ideal would be to always have fresh foods available to cook as we would for ourselves, weighing them in correct portions tailored to our dog. This type of diet is called a homemade diet and we have seen above all its benefits.

In any case, these are just the general guidelines to provide a correct and balanced homemade diet for our dog:

✓ the sources of protein most used in the preparation of the home diet are the following: turkey, beef, cod, pork, horse, sardines and chicken (only if raised without antibiotics).

83

- ✓ As for fruit and vegetables, the most popular foods include zucchinis, potatoes, carrots, green beans, zucchinis, peas and apples. Some highly appreciated extras that can be found in some recipes are sunflower oil, coconut oil and salmon oil.
- ✓ The vitamins and minerals to be integrated, on the other hand, are normally at the discretion of the veterinary nutritionist based on the dog's needs.
- ✓ The strong point of this type of feeding, as already seen above, is that the raw materials can be excluded or included at will be based on the dog's reaction to the ingredients present in the bowl, or on the basis of other needs given by any pathology.
- ✓ The recipes must be composed of over 50% real meat of organic origin and vegetables selected from local producers, as well as minerals and vitamins.
- ✓ It is necessary to use only natural ingredients of human food grade and without resorting to the use of additives and preservatives.
- ✓ Each meal must be pre-portioned according to the dog's caloric needs and cooked at a low temperature to maintain the nutrients and organoleptic properties of each ingredient.
- ✓ Finally, your homemade baby food must be served and studied for him on the basis of race, weight, sterilization, daily physical activity, build, age and gender.

Dog nutrition: foods to avoid

We always remember that the digestive system of dogs is different from ours and some foods are harmful to them. So, avoid:

- ✓ Leftovers from our dishes, especially if spicy or spicy.
- ✓ All cooked bones, especially chicken and rabbit long bones which can splinter.
- ✓ Fermented cheeses.
- ✓ Sweets and chocolate (particularly dangerous especially for puppies).
- ✓ Legumes.
- ✓ Fried.
- ✓ Fresh bread.
- ✓ Rubbish picked up on the street.

With the foods to avoid concludes our first chapter. In the second we will go into even more detail on the correct nutrition of our dog.

Chapter 2: Feeding Guidelines

This chapter covers portion control and feeding schedules, addressing specific dietary needs (such as weight loss, allergies), and tips for selecting high-quality commercial dog food.

Portion control and feeding schedules

Maintaining a healthy weight and balanced body condition are among the most important and accessible things you can do for your dog's long-term well-being. Managing your dog's weight means knowing exactly how much food he should be eating each day. That's why precise portions are so important. Weight loss, for example, begins and ends in the bowl, exercise is important, but even an active dog will gain weight if consistently overfed.

Given the immense importance of diet and the narrow margins between an ideal weight and being overweight, portion accuracy is essential. To be accurate, you need to know how many calories your dog really needs each day. For this we ask you to go and see the previous chapter: in any case, knowing your dog's caloric intake allows you to easily determine the correct total intake based on your dog's specific needs, and also makes it easy to adjust the daily calories based on your changing weight management needs. But also pay attention to the nutrients: in fact, a complete diet provides, as we have seen previously, the intake of proteins, fats, carbohydrates, vitamins, fibers and minerals in the right proportions. If we take a step towards an organic homemade diet, it is good to investigate together with a veterinary nutritionist what are the right doses and proportions for our dog since factors such as age, weight or previous illnesses can determine nutrient intakes and needs different.

For this reason, we repeat that to grow healthy and stay healthy, dogs need a balanced daily diet that contains:

✓ Proteins: about 20% of the total ration. In case of pregnancy or lactation of puppies the percentage can increase, while it decreases in older dogs.
✓ Carbohydrates: they are a rapidly available energy source and also regulate the activity of the bacterial flora.
✓ Fats: must not exceed 10%.
✓ Vitamins: especially for puppies or in case of pregnancy and breastfeeding.

- ✓ Mineral salts.

And here some tips for Dog feeding schedule:

- ✓ Puppies: they must eat 4 times a day. Then gradually it passes to 3, up to 2 in adulthood.
- ✓ At least 8 hours must pass between the two meals, to allow for complete digestion.
- ✓ One of the two meals is the main one, while the other can be lighter.
- ✓ Cookies or other treats are considered an integral part of meals.
- ✓ Food should be given at fixed and regular times, always in the same bowl and in the same place, possibly quiet and secluded.
- ✓ Wet food residues should be removed from the bowl as they oxidize easily.
- ✓ The bowl should be cleaned at each meal.
- ✓ The staple food is obviously meat, but never raw (unless you follow the BARF diet). It is then to be integrated with other foods rich in starch, such as potatoes or rice, and with vegetables (cooked), to the extent of 10-15% of the meal.
- ✓ It is important to remember that rice should not be overcooked, as prolonged cooking makes it difficult to digest.
- ✓ It is necessary that the food is in proportion to the dog's needs and perfectly balanced.
- ✓ In general, the quantities are 30 grams (1.05 oz) of food per day per kg of weight, divided between meat, rice and vegetables.
- ✓ Even fruit can be given without problems, while fish must always be cooked and obviously free of bones and thorns.
- ✓ Dry bread, much appreciated by our friends, should be given in small quantities.
- ✓ Fresh and clean water next to the bowl must never be missing.
- ✓ If kibbles are used, as well as homemade food, they can be changed from time to time, to prevent the dog from always eating the same food.
- ✓ The transition from one type of crunchy to another must always take place gradually.

Addressing specific dietary needs (e.g., weight loss, allergies, etc.)

Now let's see specifically what the food indications are based on various needs, such as age, pregnancy, weight loss or food allergies.

Feeding the puppy dog

It is important to feed our friend correctly from a puppy, also to avoid future pathologies. A balanced food must therefore include the right amount of:

✓ Protein
✓ Fat
✓ Mineral salts (especially calcium).

As soon as he is born, his mother's milk takes care of feeding him (or a specific formula milk). Then, between the sixth and seventh week, weaning begins, and the puppy can eat solid food. It is in this phase that one chooses between home-made food or industrial food (croquettes or wet).

They are both valid, the only difference is that the packaged food is already balanced to meet the nutritional needs of the puppy, while the baby food at home must be calibrated carefully. How often to feed the puppy:

✓ In the first days of life every two hours (even at night).
✓ Up to 3 months four times a day.
✓ Between 3 and 6 months three times.
✓ After 6 months twice.

The homemade diet for puppies requires a greater quantity of food (4 – 10% of body weight) than its adult diet, to be distributed several times a day. It should also be remembered that if the puppy is weaned directly on a home-made diet, it will have a hard time adapting to industrial-type foods in the future: dogs don't have many taste buds but rely on their excellent sense of smell to select food, once they get used to it. to the aromas of the unprocessed food, it will be more difficult to get him to accept the pre-packaged feed. If the process had instead taken place in reverse, a gradual shift towards the new diet is always recommended, mixing the two foods in the bowl for at least a week. Also remember to never overdo the quantities: it is true that puppies need to eat more but portions that are too large can cause even serious health problems. If you choose a food that is too rich in carbohydrates, for example, the risk for your puppy is obesity, as well as bone problems (since he is still growing) and even damage to internal organs.

Feeding the adult dog

It is important that as an adult the dog maintains muscle mass and weight, as it no longer has to grow.

Also, in this phase the choice is between homemade baby food and industrial food. I have the same considerations:

✓ home nutrition is more demanding and must be balanced (it is therefore better to consult a nutritionist), but it is more palatable. Avoid dressings that are too fatty and prefer steam cooking or boiling. Also, no to raw pork or chicken due to the risk of salmonella or diseases such as Aujeszky's disease.

✓ Industrial food. It must be said that the choice of packaged food is vast, and the price is not always synonymous with quality. What is important to know, for a correct choice, is that the croquettes or tins must contain at least 35% protein, therefore more meat than the rest.

Anyway, if you choose industrial food, avoid whose labels state:

✓ Meat derivatives. These are slaughterhouse waste (entrails, heads and legs, nails, beak and feathers)

✓ Vegetable protein extracts

✓ Meat flour (derived from the processing of animal carcasses).

Feeding the senior dog

As happens to us humans, it is also important for older dogs to change their diet. The metabolism, in fact, is no longer the same, but slowed down. Muscle mass then decreases, and physical activity is increasingly scarce.

It is therefore necessary, to avoid weight gain and obesity, to gradually reduce the daily portion of food by at least 30%.

Furthermore, it is good to choose foods that are more easily digestible and pay attention to your teeth so as not to overload your chewing. At this stage, therefore, moist foods would be preferable.

How much should a pregnant dog eat?

If your dog is in the second half of a pregnancy, her energy requirement is 1.5 times normal. In practice, for example, if you weigh 20 kg you need approximately 1762.68 kcal of energy per day.

Furthermore, compared to the standard, when a female is pregnant it is also necessary to increase her protein intake by 0.5 times. Example: Your female dog has given birth to 8 puppies and her normal weight is 20kg. To calculate her energy needs as a new mother, apply the formula as follows: 1175.12 kcal (maintenance needs) x 3 = 3525.37 kcal per day.

As with very active dogs, you don't need to increase the amount of protein so much as the daily calories.

For an overweight dog

Often, to drastically reduce energy intake and achieve the desired weight loss, the dog is given half the calories it usually eats. But a 50% diet is never recommended.

If you give your pet only half of his daily ration, even if he is overweight, he will have symptoms of nutritional deficiency after a while.

Not only. Another negative consequence is the lack of satiety: by reducing his food rations too drastically, the dog is never satisfied because his stomach is never full. Usually in these cases the dogs become insistent, they ask for food all day long, sometimes they even steal food secretly, if they have the opportunity, or they suddenly disobey, as if to protest.

That's why the best thing is to establish a dietary food plan that allows your pet to lose weight gradually and without stress. And don't forget an obvious but fundamental fact: your dog didn't put on weight all of a sudden and likewise he won't get back in shape in a few days.

Here are the breeds that are at a higher risk of becoming overweight:

- ✓ **Basset hounds**
- ✓ **Beagles**
- ✓ **Cavalier King Charles spaniel**
- ✓ **Cocker Spaniels**
- ✓ **Dachshunds**
- ✓ **Dalmatian**
- ✓ **Golden Retrievers**
- ✓ **Labrador Retrievers**

- ✓ Rottweilers

Also remember that a diet lasts for months. And even when your four-legged has reached his ideal weight, he will have to continue to eat healthily by following many of the new habits you have introduced with his diet. Otherwise, he runs the risk of gaining weight again, the famous "accordion effect" that we humans know well too.

The homemade diet, in this case, can prove to be the best solution to ensure that your dog can lose weight in a healthy and sustainable way. Feeding your dog with a healthy, balanced and personalized diet based on its characteristics is the correct solution if your dog is obese. In fact, the best way to help your dog achieve long-term well-being, and increase its life expectancy up to 3 years, is to choose natural food, not industrially processed, and in quantities proportionate to its caloric needs. The homemade diet is an excellent remedy as it generally provides proteins, carbohydrates, fats, vitamins and mineral substances. This type of diet is able to reduce the onset of pathologies and food intolerances in dogs due to the naturalness of the ingredients and the minimally invasive cooking process.

For dogs with food allergies

Food allergies in dogs manifest themselves in a sudden and complex way, causing annoying and painful symptoms such as itching, skin infections or typical cold symptoms. Preserving your dog's health, identifying the triggering causes of food intolerance, is a must to ensure longevity and a healthy lifestyle for your four-legged friend. Let's analyze in depth the symptoms, the treatment, what remedies to implement and what type of diet to administer to your trust to keep unpleasant allergies at bay. The method of choice for the diagnosis is a deprivation diet (elimination diet).

This investigation can establish a relationship between the administration of certain ingredients and the appearance of certain clinical signs.

At the same time, all the other complications must be treated, if present.

Whether it is allergy or intolerance, in both cases these diseases, albeit chronic, can be treated through an investigation into the food to which the four-legged friend is intolerant and the administration of a controlled, healthy and genuine diet.

Applying an exclusion diet to your four-legged friend, imparting a precise diet with a single type of protein for at least 6-10 weeks, will allow for the identification of the allergenic food. If within these weeks, the dog shows a physical improvement with a net decrease in symptoms, it is also possible to perform a provocation test to confirm the diagnosis. Specifically, it is appropriate to prohibit the dog from roaming freely during this period of time, as it could feed on other sources of food on the street. Avoiding the administration of extra morsels, flavored medicines, will make it possible to identify the harmful food source: in particular at mealtimes, it is advisable that the dog does not enter the dining room, as it could feed on small morsels of food that accidentally fall to the floor during the preparation of food.

Keeping a diary with all the annotations relating to the beginning of the diet written, the dates that mark the period in which a certain type of food should be administered, will help to have a complete picture of the chosen regimen. Certain data have shown that only after the tenth week of an exclusion diet, it is possible to obtain an answer and return to a "normal" but still healthy diet. By eliminating the "guilty" foods of food allergies in the daily diet, the dog will obtain useful benefits to lead a life in perfect shape. Throughout its life, it is important to guarantee the supply of vitamins and mineral salts, essential nutrients to prevent the advent of other pathologies. Hence it is advisable to choose a special diet, specific hypoallergenic foods to counteract intolerance and feed your dog in a healthy and beneficial way. This type of single-protein kibble for dogs is a light and easily digestible food: their high digestibility does not burden the intestinal tract, avoiding heaviness and diarrhea.

Tips for selecting high-quality commercial dog food

To conclude this second chapter, here is a series of tips that will help you choose the best commercial food to give to your dog (in case you want to combine it with a homemade diet).

When buying a product for your dog, the first question you need to answer is: what kind of food am I looking for? Not all dog foods are the same and it is important to know their characteristics and differences in order to juggle the countless offers on the market. Only in this way will you be able to understand if you are choosing the best food for your dog's well-being.

There is no absolute right or wrong food, but let's therefore clarify and see the differences between different types of pet food.

Complete or complementary

The first fundamental difference to identify is to check if the product you are holding is:

✓ Complete food: with a daily ration it provides all the nutrients in the quantities and proportions required by the dog. This can be dry, semi-moist or wet dog food.

✓ Complementary food: it is not sufficient to satisfy the daily ration of nutrients required by the dog. It is therefore to be used in combination with other complete foods. It can be dry, semi-moist or moist foods but also snacks.

Dry, moist and semi-humid

Having established this difference, the second aspect on which your search for the best complete feed for dogs should focus is the concentration of water inside it. On the market you will find 3 types of different products:

Dry food

contains less than 14% water. Croquettes are meant for this type of food.

Pros and cons:

✓ Practicality of administration and conservation.

✓ Nutritionally more concentrated than other types of food

✓ They have no particular disadvantages.

Dry croquettes

Semi-moist food contains between 14% and 34% water. This type of product comes in the form of soft croquettes for dogs.

Pros and cons:

✓ It retains the aroma better than dry food.

✓ Mix characteristics of dry and wet food.

✓ It has a shorter shelf life and is prone to mold growth.

Semi-moist croquettes

Wet food: contains more than 34% water. It is the type of food most appreciated by dogs.

Pros and cons:

✓ It has a more intense aroma than kibbles and is highly palatable.

✓ Less practical to store.

✓ Weight for weight less nutritious and less economical.

All types of dog foods described above are equally valid (the exception is that the vet is not agree with this).

What to watch out for

A guide to choosing dog food well should also take into account possible risk factors and slightly more particular cases. Let's see together the most common ones.

How to choose the best dog food for allergies

If your dog suffers from allergies or is particularly sensitive to one or more ingredients, it is even more important that you refer to clear labels with ingredients written explicitly and in detail. Then there are some features and wordings you should focus on to further reduce the risk of triggering intolerance symptoms.

✓ Single-protein products: choose a single-protein product if your dog is allergic to a specific type of meat (such as chicken meat) and you don't want to risk contamination. Attention: when speaking of a single protein food, the wording refers to the fact that the product contains a single protein source of animal origin. A small part of proteins also derives from cereals and legumes, whose starches necessarily serve as fillers to make the extrusion of the croquettes possible. Always keep in mind however that most allergies and intolerances are caused by low quality protein.

You should also be careful to:

✓ Grain free products: choose a grain free product (or without cereals) in case your dog is intolerant to them.

✓ Warning: grain free does not mean starch free, since starch is an essential component for making croquettes.

How to choose the best puppy food

The guidelines to follow are always the same to recognize quality products. The only further foresight added to the list is to choose a specific food for puppies (or puppy feed), which is specifically designed for this phase of a dog's life, in which a puppy's needs are very different from those of an adult dog. In addition to the maintenance requirement, i.e., the energy required to carry out normal physical activities such as eating, playing, running, one must also consider the growth requirement, aimed at providing the puppy with the nutrients necessary to make it grow in health and to allow it to develop in synergy bones and muscles proportionate to each other. As a result, puppy food should always be higher in calories and higher in protein than adult dog food. And if we talk about croquettes, these will have to be even smaller to be suitable for their mouth and teeth.

The importance of knowing how to read the label

Apart from the information on the analytical composition of the food, established by law, the parts that mainly interest us are:

✓ The composition of a product contains the list of ingredients, nutritional additives and other substances that make up the croquettes, in decreasing order of quantity.

✓ The analytical components, on the other hand, are nothing more than the nutritional table which indicates the percentages of protein, fat, crude fiber and crude ash. Don't let this last rumor scare you: raw ashes are simply the minerals and trace minerals present in the finished product.

A clear label with specified ingredients is a consumer-friendly label. That's why our labels are clear and easy to read, so you'll always be sure you know what you're feeding your pet.

Chapter 3: Homemade healthy recipes

In this third chapter, we will show you 30 recipes for homemade healthy food (divided in puppy and adult recipes 15/15).

Recipes for small size puppy

Recipe n.1

Ingredients:

- ✓ 3.5 oz of cow or lamb heart
- ✓ 1 little of white potato
- ✓ 1/4 cup of oats
- ✓ 1/4 zucchini
- ✓ 2 babu carrots
- ✓ A pinch of turmeric and rosemary
- ✓ Sunflower or corn oil

Instructions:

- ✓ Peel and mince the ingredients into little cubes, adapt for the size of your dog.
- ✓ Put the potatoes, zucchini and carrots to boil.
- ✓ Cook the meat on the griddle or in the oven employing vegetable oil. Join, at this point, all the spices to season the heart.
- ✓ Once all ingredients are well done, combine with the rest of the others, including the oats, and mash the potatoes through a fork.
- ✓ Let cool and prepare to serve.

Recipe n.2

Ingredients:

- ✓ 2 tbsp of brown rice
- ✓ 3.5 oz of salmon
- ✓ 1 raw cow femur
- ✓ 1 tbsp of cauliflower

- ✓ 1 pinch of parsley
- ✓ Sunflower oil

Instructions:
- ✓ Rinse the rice and put it to boil in plenty of water.
- ✓ Mince finely the salmon and break up the cauliflower.
- ✓ Prepare the grilled or baked salmon together with the vegetables, sprinkling with a little parsley.
- ✓ Mince the raw bone with a hand blender: remember not to cook them!
- ✓ When the rice is cooked through and the salmon and vegetables are lightly cooked, mix the chopped bone into the rice and prepare to serve.
- ✓ Join a drop of vegetable oil, mix and leave to cool.

Recipe n.3

Ingredients:
- ✓ 3.5 oz of stew meat, preferably veal
- ✓ 2 little tomatoes
- ✓ 2 baby carrots
- ✓ 1 tsp of chard
- ✓ 1 raw knuckle of veal
- ✓ Extra virgin olive oil
- ✓ thyme

Ingredients:
- ✓ Cut the carrots and chard, then grate the tomatoes.
- ✓ Put together the chopped veggies and add them to the pan and cook them for a few minutes.
- ✓ Add the cubed meat and wait until it is cooked through.

Recipe n.4

Ingredients:
- ✓ 3.5 oz of chicken or turkey meat
- ✓ 2 tsp of white rice

- ✓ 2 little size eggs
- ✓ 1/2 yoghurt
- ✓ 2 tbsp of asparagus
- ✓ Corn vegetable oil

Instructions:
- ✓ Boil the two eggs in a pan and remove them when they are completely cooked.
- ✓ Grate the eggs.
- ✓ Crush the egg shells
- ✓ Chop the chicken into small cubes.
- ✓ Boil water in another pan.
- ✓ Cook the asparagus in a pan and add rice and boiling water.
- ✓ Constantly mix asparagus and rice to prevent sticking.
- ✓ Add more water as the rice absorbs it.
- ✓ When the rice is cooked, join chicken pieces to it and the grated egg.
- ✓ Finally, don't forget to add half a yogurt and the chopped eggshell.

Recipe n.4

Ingredients:
- ✓ 3.5 oz of veal for stew
- ✓ 2 tbsp of sweet potatoes
- ✓ 1 spoonful of brewer's yeast
- ✓ Extra virgin olive oil
- ✓ A pinch of thyme
- ✓ 2 tbsp of kefir

Instructions:
- ✓ Dice the sweet potato and put them to boil.
- ✓ Lightly cook the meat in the pan, adding the olive oil and thyme.
- ✓ Once the sweet potatoes are cooked, chop them, joining the kefir and brewer's yeast.
- ✓ Add the meat, breaking it up.
- ✓ Mix all the ingredients and form a patty. Let him rest.

- ✓ You can end cooking in the oven or let it rest at room temperature. Once done it, serve to your dog.

Recipes for medium size puppy

Recipe n.1

Ingredients:
- ✓ 5.29 oz of chicken
- ✓ 5.29 oz of white potato
- ✓ 1/2 cup oats
- ✓ 1/2 zucchini
- ✓ 3 carrots
- ✓ Sunflower or corn oil

Instructions:
- ✓ Cut the vegetables into very small cubes (remember that he is a puppy not used to large bites).
- ✓ Then put the freshly cut potatoes, zucchini and carrots to boil. Separately, blanch the chicken and cut it into small pieces when cooked.
- ✓ Combine everything in a pan with a drizzle of oil, a spoonful of water and half a cup of oats and finish cooking. Let all cooling and offer to the puppy at room temperature.

Recipe n.2

Ingredients:
- ✓ 1 cup of turkey
- ✓ 1 fennel
- ✓ 2 carrots
- ✓ Extra virgin olive oil
- ✓ Thyme

Instructions:
- ✓ Wash and then cut the carrots and fennel into small pieces.
- ✓ Cook them for a few minutes in boiling water.

- ✓ Add the turkey meat cut into small cubes and a sprig of thyme.
- ✓ Cook until cooked through.
- ✓ Mix everything and add a drizzle of extra virgin olive oil.
- ✓ Let cooling and serve to the puppy.

Recipe n.3

Ingredients:
- ✓ 5.39 oz of lamb meat
- ✓ 3 tbsp of white rice
- ✓ 1 egg
- ✓ 1/2 yogurt
- ✓ 3 tbsp of chard
- ✓ Corn vegetable oil

Instructions:
- ✓ Start by washing the rice and then cook it in plenty of water.
- ✓ Do the same with the eggs, cook them in a pan and remove when cooked.
- ✓ Grate the eggs and crush the shells.
- ✓ Meanwhile, in another saucepan, blanch the lamb cut into small cubes.
- ✓ In another pan, blanch the chard and add the rice.
- ✓ Once the rice is completely cooked add the lamb and the grated egg and only at the end add the yogurt and the chopped eggshell.
- ✓ Let cooling and serve to the puppy.

Recipe n.4

Ingredients:
- ✓ 3 tbsp of brown rice
- ✓ 1 cup and ½ of cod
- ✓ 3 tbsp of zucchini
- ✓ 1 pinch of cilantro
- ✓ Sunflower oil

Instructions:

- ✓ Boil brown rice in plenty of water, but don't forget to rinse it first.
- ✓ Cut the cod and zucchini into small cubes.
- ✓ Bake the cod and zucchini in the oven, sprinkle with some cilantro leaves.
- ✓ When the rice is completely cooked, the cod and zucchini are half cooked, add everything.
- ✓ Cool and then serve, adding a drop of vegetable oil.

Recipe n.5

Ingredients:

- ✓ ¼ cup of brown rice
- ✓ 1 cup and ½ of salmon
- ✓ 1/2 yogurt
- ✓ Extra virgin olive oil
- ✓ Half a potato
- ✓ Half a zucchini
- ✓ Half a carrot

Instructions

- ✓ Wash the rice and cook it in plenty of water.
- ✓ Wash and cut the potatoes, zucchini and carrot.
- ✓ Place everything on a tray and cook in the oven together with the piece of salmon.
- ✓ When the rice is done and the salmon and veggies are almost cooked, combine everything in the rice pot and mix with a drizzle of oil and half a jar of yogurt.
- ✓ Leave to cool and serve to the puppy.

Recipes for big size puppy

Recipe n.1

Ingredients

- ✓ 1 cup and 2 tbsp of Cooked lean minced beef
- ✓ 1 tsp of Corn oil: 2 g
- ✓ 1 tsp Omega 3 oil
- ✓ Complete supplement for dogs: according to the manufacturer's instructions

Instructions:

- ✓ In a pan with a little water, cook the meat over a low heat without reaching the boiling point (160°F for 8-10 minutes. This way the meat is sanitized but does not lose its nutritional properties).
- ✓ Leave to cool, add the supplement and oil and split into small portions.
- ✓ Keep in the fridge.
- ✓ Serve the single portions at a temperature of about 98°F.

Recipe n.2

Ingredients

- ✓ 1 cup of Basmati brown rice
- ✓ ½ cup Frozen minestrone mix
- ✓ 1 potato
- ✓ 3 cups of Water
- ✓ 2 tbsp extra virgin olive oil

Instructions:

- ✓ The preparation is really very simple: there are only three simple ingredients to which a potato will be added at the end of cooking.
- ✓ Bring the water to the boil and pour in the brown Basmati rice, without adding salt.
- ✓ Put the still frozen minestrone in the water.
- ✓ Cook over low heat until the rice is well cooked.
- ✓ Meanwhile boil the potato.
- ✓ Once the potato is cooked, peel it and mash it with a fork.
- ✓ Join it to the rice once cooked, obtaining a creamy dish.
- ✓ Leave to cool and serve with a drizzle of extra virgin olive oil.
- ✓ Possibly embellish the dish with minced turkey or beef to add with the heat off.

Recipe n.3

Ingredients:

- ✓ 1 cup minced chicken meat
- ✓ ¼ cup of cooked brown rice

- ✓ ¼ cup of green beans

Instructions:
- ✓ First, cook the chicken meat in a pan.
- ✓ Once fully cooked, drain the fat.
- ✓ Add the cooked brown rice, mix well and put aside.
- ✓ Cut the beans into small pieces.
- ✓ Put them in a pot with water, bring to a boil.
- ✓ Leave to cook until the veggies result tender (about 15-20 minutes).
- ✓ Add the veggies to the meat mixture and put together.
- ✓ Allow the meal to cool for about an hour before serving it to your dog.

Recipe n.4

Ingredients:
- ✓ 1 cup ground beef
- ✓ 1 chicken liver
- ✓ 1/3 cup of cooked basmati rice
- ✓ 1/2 cup mixed vegetables (no onion and no garlic)

Instructions:
- ✓ Chop the vegetables in a mixer.
- ✓ Add all ingredients (beef, rice, vegetables, greens and liver) to a pan and mix.
- ✓ Pour enough water to cover all the ingredients and then boil everything for about 2 hours.
- ✓ Then divide the mixture into several separate portions and freeze in plastic bags.
- ✓ When serving, add a teaspoon of olive oil (not always) once or twice a week.

Recipe n.5

Ingredients:
- ✓ ¼ cup rice
- ✓ 1 cup of salmon
- ✓ 1/2 yogurt
- ✓ Extra virgin olive oil

- ✓ 1 potato
- ✓ 1 zucchini

Instructions:
- ✓ First, wash the rice and cook it in plenty of water.
- ✓ Wash and cut the potatoes and zucchini.
- ✓ Place everything on a tray and cook in the oven together with the piece of salmon.
- ✓ As soon as the rice is done and the salmon and veggies are almost cooked, combine everything in the rice pot and mix with a drizzle of oil and half a jar of yogurt.
- ✓ Leave to cool and serve to the puppy.

Recipes for small size adult

Recipe n.1

Ingredients:
- ✓ Half a glass of hot water
- ✓ Chicken or beef broth
- ✓ 1 pack of dry yeast
- ✓ 1 small glass of tomato juice/preserve
- ✓ 1 cup of wheat germs
- ✓ 1 cup of durum wheat flour

Instructions:
- ✓ Put the broth in a bowl.
- ✓ Add the yeast and leave to rest for about five minutes, or when the yeast is completely dissolved.
- ✓ Add the tomato juice, half the flour and the wheat germs and mix to form a soft batter.
- ✓ Gradually add the durum wheat flour and mix the mixture with your hands.
- ✓ Divide the dough into 4 parts.
- ✓ Roll out each piece to 0,39 inches thick on a floured surface.
- ✓ Cut the mixture into the desired cookie shape.
- ✓ Bake at 338°F for 1 hour, then turn off the oven and let the biscuits dry for about 1 hour.

- ✓ Store in airtight container.
- ✓ Always serve at room temperature.

Recipe n.2

Ingredients:
- ✓ 1 cup and half of boiled chicken
- ✓ 1/3 cup of cooked brown rice
- ✓ 1/3 cup of mixed steamed vegetables (carrots, green beans, peas, spinach)
- ✓ 4 tablespoons unsalted chicken broth

Instructions:
- ✓ Boil the cup and half of chicken in water.
- ✓ Drain the water, join the broth to it and the cooked rice.
- ✓ Cook for a few minutes and then add the mixed vegetables.
- ✓ Continue to simmer for 10 minutes.
- ✓ Let it cool and serve cold.
- ✓ Store in the fridge for maximum 4 days.

Recipe n.3

Ingredients:
- ✓ 1 cup and half of minced salmon
- ✓ 1/3 cup of cooked brown rice
- ✓ 2 oz of mixed boiled vegetables
- ✓ 3-4 tablespoons of water

Instructions:
- ✓ Cook the salmon in a pan by adding the water, and then the rice and boiled vegetables.
- ✓ Add water if necessary.
- ✓ Cook for about 15 minutes on low heat.
- ✓ Leave to cool and serve cold.
- ✓ Store in the fridge for maximum 4 days.

Recipe n.4

Ingredients:

- ✓ 1 cup minced meat (turkey, chicken, lamb)
- ✓ 3 tbsp of cooked rice
- ✓ 1 oz of green beans

Instructions:

- ✓ As first thing to do. let the meat cook in a pan.
- ✓ When fully cooked, drain the fat.
- ✓ Join the cooked rice and put together.
- ✓ Set aside. At the same time, split the beans into small pieces.
- ✓ Put them in a pot with water, bring to a boil.
- ✓ Leave to cook until the veggies are tender enough (about 15-20 minutes).
- ✓ Add the vegetables to the meat mixture and mix.
- ✓ Allow the meal to cool for about an hour before serving it to your small size dog.

Recipe n.5

Ingredients:

- ✓ ½ cup ground beef
- ✓ ½ cup of cooked brown rice
- ✓ ½ cup mixed vegetables (no onion)
- ✓ 1 chicken liver

Instructions:

- ✓ Chop the vegetables in a mixer.
- ✓ Add all ingredients (beef, rice, vegetables, greens and liver) to a pan and mix.
- ✓ Pour some water able to cover all the ingredients and then boil everything for about 2 hours.
- ✓ Then divide the mixture into several separate portions and freeze in plastic bags.
- ✓ When serving, add a teaspoon of olive oil (not always) once or twice a week

Recipes for medium size adult

Recipe n.1

Ingredients:

- ✓ 2 cups of chicken or ground beef
- ✓ 2 cups of frozen mixed vegetables (no onion)
- ✓ ½ cup and half of rice
- ✓ Water to cover the ingredients in the pan Broth

Instructions:

- ✓ Place the minced meat in a large pot, cover with the water and bring to a boil.
- ✓ Add the vegetables, rice and more water if needed (to cover) and beef stock.
- ✓ Other ingredients can also be added as desired.
- ✓ Turn the ingredients until the rice is cooked through, pouring water if necessary.
- ✓ Leave to cool and serve (or divide the mixture into portions and freeze until ready to use).

Recipe n.2

Ingredients:

- ✓ 1.1 lbs of any type of meat
- ✓ 1 finely chopped carrot
- ✓ 1 small potato cooked and finely chopped (in small quantities it does not cause problems for the dog, if the potato is larger, use only a part (it also depends on the size of the dog of course).
- ✓ 1 celery stalk finely chopped

Instructions:

- ✓ Put all the ingredients in a large saucepan.
- ✓ Cover with water and mix.
- ✓ Place the lid on the saucepan and place in the microwave at maximum power for 4 minutes and then at medium power for another 4 minutes.
- ✓ Check the doneness periodically, maybe it takes longer, it depends a lot on the oven.
- ✓ Serve cold. (Let cool at least 1 hour)

Recipe n.3

Ingredients:

- ✓ 1/3 cup of powdered milk
- ✓ 1/2 teaspoon salt
- ✓ 1 egg, well battered
- ✓ 1 / 2 glass of water
- ✓ 2 cups of flour
- ✓ 1 and 1/2 tsp of brown sugar
- ✓ 1 homogenized meat-based baby (without onion)

Instructions:

- ✓ Mix all the ingredients well.
- ✓ Roll out on a surface with some flour about 0,39 inches thick of the compound.
- ✓ Cut the biscuits into any shape you like.
- ✓ Bake in the oven at 356° for 20 minutes.
- ✓ Let them cool, perhaps leaving them in the oven to dry.
- ✓ Store in an airtight container

Recipe n.4

Ingredients:

- ✓ 1 cup cooked brown rice
- ✓ ½ cup of lean beef
- ✓ 2 teaspoons of lard
- ✓ 1/2 of chopped mixed vegetables (no onion)

Instructions:

- ✓ Place all the ingredients in a saucepan (water as required) and cook until the rice is cooked. Mix.
- ✓ Add a spoonful of olive oil at the end of cooking.
- ✓ Instead of beef you can also use other types of meat (lamb, turkey, chicken).
- ✓ Serve warm.

Recipe n.5

Ingredients:

- ✓ 2 chicken thighs – or white meat
- ✓ 1 celery stalk – thickly sliced
- ✓ 1 carrot – peeled and cut in half
- ✓ 1 cup of rice – raw

Instructions:

- ✓ Place the chicken thighs in a large pot.
- ✓ Cover with cold water (5 -6 glasses).
- ✓ Add the carrots and celery to the water.
- ✓ Cover and cook over low heat about 2 hours, until chicken is tender.
- ✓ Join also the rice, cover and let cook over low heat for about thirty minutes.
- ✓ You can also wait until the rice is cooked through and most of the water has been absorbed.
- ✓ Remove soup from heat.
- ✓ Take out the chicken meat and remove the bones.
- ✓ Return the boneless chicken to the pot.
- ✓ Mix well for about 2 minutes over low heat.
- ✓ Serve cold. Store in the fridge or freeze in portions.

Recipes for big size adult

Recipe n.1

Ingredients

- ✓ 1 cup and ½ of rice
- ✓ Grated carrots (to taste)
- ✓ 3 tbsp Parsley
- ✓ 1 cup of Peas
- ✓ 1 cooked sweet potato

Instructions:

- ✓ Combine the rice, carrots, parsley, and peas in a saucepan.
- ✓ Cook as you normally do for cooking rice, do not use salt.

- ✓ While the rice is cooking, boil the sweet potato in water.
- ✓ When it is tender (if a knife passes through the potato without forcing, it is ready), remove it from the water, peel it and mash it (like mashed potatoes).
- ✓ Add the mashed potatoes to the mixture in the pot and mix all the ingredients well. Serve hot.
- ✓ P.S. If you want to add some meat to your meal, I recommend using very lean ground beef or turkey – I prefer turkey, as dogs don't need a lot of "red meat" in their diet. Simply add a pound of ground beef to the base mixture.

Recipe n.2

Ingredients
- ✓ 2.2 lbs minced meat (turkey, lamb or rabbit)
- ✓ 2 cups barley, (or brown rice or millet) normal cooking
- ✓ 1 cup of raw vegetables chopped with a mixer (cabbage, cooked potatoes, carrots, green beans)
- ✓ A cup of olive oil

Instructions:
- ✓ Brown the meat and mix with the cereals and vegetables.
- ✓ Leave to cool completely before serving to your dog.
- ✓ The oil is added at the end of cooking. I usually make a large batch of this and then store it in the freezer in separate bags per serving.
- ✓ So, when you need it, you can defrost the bags!
- ✓ Once a week, add a freshly beaten egg to the mixture.
- ✓ The recommended portions are 1.8 oz for every 10kg (your dog's weight) twice a day.

Recipe n.3

Ingredients
- ✓ 6 chicken legs
- ✓ 2.2 lbs frozen mixed vegetables (no onion)
- ✓ 10.5 oz oatmeal or brown rice

Instructions:
- ✓ Boil the chicken in water until the meat is soft and it is easy to separate it from the bones.
- ✓ If you are using a pressure cooker, after cooking you should be able to mash the bones with your fingers due to how soft they are.
- ✓ At this point remove the chicken from the water.
- ✓ Leave to cool.
- ✓ Separate the flesh, skin, cartilage from the bones.
- ✓ Check meat bones carefully.
- ✓ Put frozen vegetables in blender. Add chicken stock (cooking and puree. Cook oatmeal and/or rice in remaining water. (This could be done at the same time as cooking chicken.)
- ✓ Add the chicken (boneless), vegetables and oats or rice. If the "minestrone" is too thick, add water.
- ✓ Let it cool before serving. Store in the refrigerator. Proportion the amount of food according to your dog's weight.

Recipe n.4

Ingredients:
- ✓ 3 cups cooked brown rice
- ✓ 3 cups grated vegetables
- ✓ ½ cup cottage cheese
- ✓ 2 tbsp of nutritional yeast
- ✓ 2 tbsp of whole milk
- ✓ 2 tbsp of grated cheese

Instructions:
- ✓ Combine and mix the first 4 ingredients (flour, grated vegetables, ricotta and baking powder) in a saucepan.
- ✓ Then pour the milk and sprinkle with grated cheese.
- ✓ Bake for about 15 minutes at 356°F or until the cheese melts and turns slightly orange.
- ✓ Serve cold.

Recipe n.4

Ingredients:
- ✓ 1.1 lbs of pasta for dogs
- ✓ 1.1 lbs of brown rice
- ✓ 4.4 lbs chicken (thigh)
- ✓ 1.1 lbs of chicken livers
- ✓ 3 cups of mixed vegetables (no onion)

Instructions:
- ✓ Put the liver and rice in a saucepan, add the water and rice in a ratio of 2-1 (2 cups of water to 1 cup of rice), bring to a boil.
- ✓ Lower the heat and cook for 40 minutes.
- ✓ Bake the chicken (a few spices) in the oven at 375°F for 90 – 120 minutes.
- ✓ Boil the water in a large pot then add the pasta. Cook 8 -10 minutes.
- ✓ Arrange the drained pasta into the pan with the liver and rice and mix the ingredients well. The pot should be big enough to have all the ingredients inside of it.
- ✓ Pour the vegetables together with the other ingredients.
- ✓ Debone the chicken and put it in the pot along with everything else. Cook for a few minutes on low heat.
- ✓ Slit into portions and freeze. Let rest inside until ready to use.

With these healthy recipes for dogs of all ages and sizes, we have finished our fourth guide. In the fifth book we will focus on the hygiene and health of our dog.

PART 5: HEALTHY DOG GUIDE

Introduction

This fifth book will be totally dedicated to the hygiene and the health of our dogs. There will be so many ways to do it and how to recognize and prevent dog diseases and injuries.

Chapter 1: Grooming and Hygiene

Maintaining your dog's hygiene is a fundamental part of being a responsible dog master. This chapter covers bathing and brushing techniques, dental care and oral hygiene, and nail trimming and other grooming tasks.

Bathing and brushing techniques

The care and beauty of the dog pass through attention to dog hygiene. The cleanliness and hygiene of the dog pass, in turn, through the cleaning of the eyes, ears, teeth, paws and fur.

Our dog's skin and coat are both in fact the mirror of his well-being and therefore it is extremely important to take care of your dog's coat throughout the year, not just during the seasonal moulting period. But how does the dog moult? The moult takes place during the period of climate change generally twice a year and varies in intensity and duration depending on the breed and lifestyle. The hair does not all fall out at the same time, but progressively from the back of the body towards the front. The moult depends on the photoperiod, i.e., the hours of exposure to light, which is why dogs that live outdoors have a shorter and more regular moult than dogs that live in apartments. The latter are exposed to electric light, to the radiator or to the air conditioner and consequently lose their hair almost all year round with an accentuation of the phenomenon at the seasonal change (thickening of the undercoat with the arrival of winter and thinning in spring).

The skin is also a dynamic organ composed of multiple layers of cells that mature and result in the formation of horny scales. In a healthy dog, this cell turnover takes about 22 days. However, a visible buildup of flaking products (dandruff) is not normal.

Warning signs that should never be underestimated are therefore excessive hair loss, the presence of alopecia (hairless) areas, the appearance of crusts or dandruff, reddened skin and itching.

Why is brushing important? Brushing techniques

Among the most common causes of dull or sparse hair is the lack of regular brushing.

A first reason to brush it for those who live with a dog at home certainly have it under their eyes for most of the year: dogs lose hair. Much.

113

Who hasn't happened to find themselves under the bed, in the corners of the corridor or along the baseboards of furry clouds that roll here and there at the slightest breath of wind like the infamous rolling bushes in western films? We arm ourselves with vacuum cleaners, but the next day they reappear.

Brushing your dog regularly will help you worry less about these clouds of fur.

This practice should be daily especially in long-haired dogs. Even infrequent or, on the contrary, too frequent washing or the use of aggressive or non-specific veterinary products can harm the health of the hair which is brittle with the consequent appearance of various types of dermatitis. Brushing will also allow you to closely inspect the coat and skin of the animal, noting for example if fleas or ticks are present and acting accordingly.

Another thing that brushing your dog will help you avoid is the possible presence of fora sacks, the mature ears of grasses, which can stick to the dog's ears, muzzle and paws, risking causing infections as they penetrate deeply.

It is therefore advisable to brush almost daily also to loosen the knots in long-haired or curly-haired subjects (1-2 times a week in short-haired dogs) and a wash in the grooming department to be carried out 2-3 times a year to clean without attack the skin while maintaining the natural sebum layer that protects our dog from atmospheric agents.

Also, for this reason it is totally wrong to shear dogs during the summer as their thermoregulation is compromised. Pay particular attention to spring and autumn, seasons in which it becomes essential to remove the undercoat.

Removing the undercoat of the dog in unsuitable periods in fact means risking ruining the characteristics of the coat of the breed.

The undercoat is removed not with the hands but precisely with the carder (the brush alone cannot do it). The carder should not be used with circular movements (which would knot the hair), but from the base to the tips. It is essential, in this case, to stretch the skin with one hand and brush with the other so that the skin is not stressed.

The movement to be used is indifferent, the important thing is that the brush or carder opens the coat in every single point until you can see the skin.

You need to brush from the base to the tip, that is, brushing the ends alone is not enough.

It is important to brush everywhere and every part. Not only this: you should insist on the portions where the dog generates more undercoat or knots more.

These portions are: on the back, in the lengths of the ears, near collars and harnesses, , back, and so on...There are different types of brushes and you have to choose the most suitable type according to the type of hair to avoid breaking it and ruining the coat. Those with soft bristles are not painful but inefficient. Metallic ones detangle more.

The carder is a fine-toothed metal tool for thick coats to remove excess undercoat especially for long-haired and large-sized dogs.

Obviously a healthy and balanced diet is essential for the well-being of the coat and there are various ad hoc formulated supplements on the market with essential fatty acids and biotin which act on the skin to restore the correct production of sebum and make the skin and hair healthier softer.

Bathing: why it is so important and techniques

Washing your dog is a fundamental habit if you care not only about the appearance, but also about the health of your four-legged friend. In fact, it allows you to clean the animal of accumulated dirt, get rid of dead hair and eliminate any parasites that lurk in the coat.

Anyway, for what about bath and grooming it's important that your dog is clean, especially if he spends a lot of time on the sofa and bed at home with you. The dog can be taken to a specialized shop at about six months of age, where it will be treated with specific products and tools.

From frequency to the most suitable products, here are 8 tips on how to wash your dog correctly: with a little patience and organization, you can transform bath time into a pleasant experience for both of you. First, let us tell you that bathing our four-legged friend is a good hygienic rule, to be carried out with a certain regularity. Theories about how often to wash your dog are often conflicting. In general, however, if there are no needs, once a month may be sufficient. Too frequent baths in fact risk altering the lipid layer naturally present on the dog's skin, exposing it to the aggression of external agents such as parasites and bacteria. But now, let's see these eight tips together:

1. Give your dog time to adjust to water

Before bathing your dog, especially if it's his first experience, give him time to gradually familiarize himself with the water. A good technique consists in placing the animal in an empty tub: in the meantime, you entertain it with a toy, caress it and address it in a reassuring tone of voice, so that it associates the bath with an experience agreeable.

When the dog is sufficiently relaxed, a little warm water is run and the tub is filled, stopping when the level reaches knee height.

The ideal is to do everything calmly, giving the animal breaks, moments of play and gratification. The dog should be bath trained since he is a puppy, but it is good to avoid washing him before 5 weeks of age: in the first few days of life his immune defenses are not fully developed, and he risks being more exposed to health problems.

2. Start with a good brush

To prepare your dog for washing, brush him carefully beforehand. The removal of the most superficial dirt, dead hair and any tangles will favor the subsequent penetration of the shampoo, making its cleansing effect more effective. To keep a soft and fluffy coat, you can use specific oils or balms, to be applied every 2-3 weeks.

3. Protect the dog's ears

Any stagnation of water in the ear canal can favor the proliferation of infectious agents. To prevent this from happening, protect your dog's ears with cotton balls. Secure them so that they are snug, but don't push them too deeply.

4. Wet the dog from the neck down

When washing your dog, carefully avoid the head and muzzle. The risk is that the water may accidentally end up in the animal's ears and that the shampoo will cause itchy eyes. Then wet the dog starting from the neck, continuing the abdomen, legs, back and tail. Make sure the coat is well soaked with water; in animals with long and thick hair, this operation can take some time.

5. Use the right shampoo

Always use a specific shampoo for dogs. The pH of canine skin is around 7, therefore more basic than that of our skin. As a result, shampoos for human use are too aggressive for the animal's skin and their improper use could cause redness, irritation and dermatitis. If your dog is particularly sensitive, you can choose a special cleaner that is completely free of perfumes, fragrances and artificial additives.

6. Clean the muzzle separately

As already mentioned, it is not advisable to wet the dog's muzzle directly. To clean it, you can use a damp towel, being careful not to stick it in your ears. If your skin has wrinkles and folds, be sure to clean these furrows thoroughly as well.

7. Always rinse the coat carefully

After washing, it is important to remove all shampoo residues. Then rinse the dog's coat carefully, until the water runs clear. This operation may require a little patience, especially if your four-legged friend has thick or curly hair, but you will avoid the risk of skin irritations and pH imbalances.

8. Do not skip the drying step

If the dog stays damp, he can easily catch a cold. It is always better to dry it well, first by wrapping it and dabbing it with a soft towel, and then completing the operation with a hairdryer. Always keep in mind that canine skin is more sensitive than ours and check that the air is not too hot to avoid burns. If your dog has very long or shaggy hair, brush it before drying it will be easier to manage and you will avoid the formation of knots or tangles.

When and how to clean the ears in dogs

Ear cleaning must be performed with suitable products called cerumenolytics, i.e., capable of emulsifying lipids and dissolving earwax. Long ears should be folded back to expose the ear canal making it easier to introduce the cleansing product. This is followed by a delicate massage at the base of the ear and, if necessary, the excess of wax and product must be dried with a tissue.

The shaking of the ears by the dog will facilitate the removal of the earwax.

In case of ear infections, cleaning must be performed daily by the owner before applying the therapeutic drops to facilitate and enhance their action. In predisposed subjects it is advisable to clean more or less constantly (3 times a week) to avoid recurrences. In all other subjects it may be sufficient to clean once a week.

Eye hygiene: how to prevent eye diseases

Even eye cleaning is not a simple aesthetic act, but a good daily habit that allows you to remove abundant secretions and reduce the risk of eye infections.

Furthermore, constant hygiene reduces the irritating effects of dust and environmental pollutants and counteracts the abundant tearing which causes the dark color often seen in white-coated dogs.

It is advisable not to use tap water or "do-it-yourself" remedies (water and chamomile) which often do not maintain sterility. Better to use prepackaged solutions (including 0.9% NaCl saline) or eye wipes. It is good practice to use a clean wipe for each eye to avoid contamination.

117

For daily hygiene it is also advisable to use wet wipes for dogs to clean the paws and genital area after the walk. Alternatively, you can opt for the use of water and Amuchina diluted at 3% to disinfect the indicated areas.

Some simple rules to follow every day

Now let's see instead the hygiene rules that must be followed daily:

1. Clean the paws after returning from walks. Every time you take your dog to the park, it is a good idea to clean his paws with wet wipes before returning to the house.

2. Clean their eyes. The eyes are, as we have explained above, very delicate and must be kept clean by eliminating all impurities and secretions.

3. Clean their private parts. During the day, if you keep your faithful companion at home, it is a good idea to wash your private parts thoroughly with wet wipes.

Dental care and oral hygiene

Now let's move on to our dog's oral hygiene. A healthy mouth, as for us humans, is the result of careful dental care for your dog, on which the well-being of the whole body also depends.

Oral hygiene, in fact, plays an important role in the health of the dog and is therefore an aspect that should never be underestimated: the accumulation of plaque and tartar does not just cause yellowing of the teeth and bad breath, but it is often responsible for more serious ailments, such as inflammation of the gums, cavities and abscesses. If neglected, these problems risk causing infections, which, in some cases, could even prove life-threatening to the animal. But, brushing your dog's teeth is an important hygiene rule, but not always appreciated by our four-legged friends. The suggestion is to give the animal time to get used to the cleaning operations and introduce this habit gradually and without forcing it, until it becomes a daily appointment. Remember that every dog is different, so it will be essential to respect their rhythms. When the dog is not used to having his teeth cleaned, gauze or a cotton stick can be used if the dog is small. To be able to do this, if the dog gets agitated and doesn't want to be touched, one of the tips is to pass the support over the croquettes to make the action palatable, so that he gets used to letting his teeth be brushed. To encourage him to collaborate more, you can use prizes and rewards, but above all, give him lots of cuddles and praise.

Before asking yourself how to clean your dog's teeth, know that this is a habit that must be done already when your four-legged friend is a puppy to facilitate the simplicity of the action.

In this way it will be possible to avoid wasting time or hurting cleaning the teeth because the animal gets agitated and does not stay still.

But this is not enough. While it is true that the owner can take care of the dog's oral hygiene, it is always better to have him checked periodically by the vet to evaluate his general state of health and his mouth in more detail.

Scaling and polishing, depending on the case and the character of the individual specimen, are often performed under anesthesia to ensure more thorough cleaning of the teeth.

Anyway, to find out how to properly clean your four-legged friend's mouth, take a look at the following instructions: in six steps you'll find out how to clean your dog's teeth perfectly.

1. STEP 1: arm yourself with the right tools

First, make sure you have the right equipment for cleaning your dog's teeth. You will need:

✓ Dog toothbrush: Get a dog toothbrush. Choose a model with soft bristles, equipped with a sufficiently long and ergonomic handle and in a format suitable for the size of the animal. Alternatively, opt for a finger brush, to be worn like a thimble.

✓ Toothpaste for dogs: Use a toothpaste specially formulated for dogs. On the market you can find many kinds, even with particularly attractive tastes. Never replace the specific toothpaste with those for human use: almost all contain fluorine, a highly toxic substance for dogs.

✓ A lot of patience and a little strategy.

2. STEP 2: let your dog get familiar with the toothpaste.

Before you start brushing your dog's teeth, allow your pet to taste some of the toothpaste. In this way, he will be able to get used to the taste of the product and will accept it more willingly when you present it to him on the toothbrush. The most effective technique is to apply a small amount of toothpaste to one finger, then present it to the dog; when he has smelled and licked the product, you can gently spread the remaining part in the animal's mouth, passing your finger over the teeth and gums.

3. STEP 3: allow the dog to get to know the toothbrush.

Before putting the toothbrush in your dog's mouth, give your pet time to inspect it. Once he's familiar with the tool, you can allow your dog to lick some of the toothpaste straight off the toothbrush.

4. STEP 4: brush your teeth little at a time.

Gently insert your fingers into your dog's mouth so that he gets used to the presence of a foreign body, without having the instinct to bite. Once he appears relaxed enough, try brushing a few teeth. The ideal is to start with the canines, which are longer and easier to clean; then you can move on to the back teeth (molars and premolars). Brush the incisors only at the end, as these are the most sensitive teeth.

5. STEP 5: clean the outer arches.

   Once the dog has become familiar with the toothbrush, you can dedicate yourself to the actual cleaning of the teeth. Apply a small amount of toothpaste to the bristles and begin very carefully brushing the outer surfaces of the teeth on both arches. First make small rotary movements, then finish cleaning by brushing vertically, from top to bottom, to remove plaque between the various interstitial spaces. Remember to maintain an angle of about 45° between the toothbrush and the surface of the teeth, so as to easily reach the gum line as well.

6. STEP 6: continue with internal surfaces.

   Once your pet is used to cleaning the outside of the teeth, you can complete the job by switching to the inside area. Place your hand on the top of the dog's face, then gently lift his lips to open his mouth. Once you have access to the oral cavity, scrub a small area of the inner arch, always moving slowly and gently. If during cleaning you notice loose teeth, abnormal bleeding or areas of the mouth that show particular sensitivity, it is always advisable to contact your vet.

How to take care of dog's teeth with oral hygiene tools?

In addition to dental health, it is always necessary for our dog to have correct and continuous oral hygiene. It is not always easy to understand how to perform correct canine oral hygiene, but there are many tools on the market that can help you in this endeavor.

The allies of dental hygiene, as well as toothbrush and toothpaste, of dogs are:

✓ Chewable sticks, bones and sticks for dogs can be found in all shapes and types on the market. They essentially allow you to clean your pet's teeth while he uses them for recreational purposes by chewing on them and playing with them. Precisely for this reason they are also suitable for dogs less accustomed to having their hands in their mouths from their owner or the vet. Choose them with ingredients of natural and vegetable origin such as cellulose, also useful for intestinal well-being thanks to the contribution of fibers.

✓ Other functional foods for cleaning teeth are all types of dry food such as biscuits but also croquettes. Of the former there are various types on the market, some with a specific anti-tartar shape (they can be recognized by the particular knurling). Oral hygiene supplements for dogs, usually based on functional active ingredients to fight plaque and bad breath in young and old puppies.

✓ Oral hygiene wipes: a less known and used tool than the previous ones but which you can think of using if your dog is particularly patient. They usually slip over your finger and allow for a gentle but deep rub of your dog's teeth and gums.

With these tools you can guarantee more than enough cleaning of the oral cavity, but there may be special cases in which all this is not enough. For example, if your dog's gums become inflamed or even infected, a dog teeth cleaning (or scaling) may be necessary. Obviously, the latter must be done by the vet who will also establish the cost of oral hygiene practice. Always him, he will tell you how often to brush your dog's teeth to avoid tartar and bad breath problems.

Nail trimming and other grooming tasks

Dog nails need regular care, just like ours. Unless your dog spends a lot of time stepping on hard surfaces, which naturally file their nails, you will need to trim and file them yourself.

If the nails touch the floor or bend to the side, you should know that they can cause the dog to adopt unnatural gaits with possible damage to diseases. Dogs' nails grow and if they are not trimmed periodically, they could bend and even stick inside the pads of the paws, creating easily infected wounds.

When to cut your dog's nails?

Usually, the dog's nails should be short and not touch the ground when the dog puts his paw down. If you hear the impact of nails on the ground (similar to a tic), it means that they are too long and must be cut as soon as possible.

Different factors influence nail growth, but the main ones are the environment and lifestyle. The nails of dogs that live in the city and walk on asphalt, or those of dogs that work outdoors on hard and rough terrain, will stay shorter for longer. On the other hand, the nails of a dog who lives mainly indoors or who runs on relatively soft surfaces wear less and therefore will grow longer more quickly. Get your dog used to nail clipping from an early age: it's much easier to establish a routine as a puppy than as an adult. However, if trimming your dog's nails stresses you out or if you just don't feel like it, talk to a professional dog groomer or your vet - they'll take care of it for you at a reasonable cost. If you have any other concerns (for example, if a nail seems to be bothering your dog), contact your vet.

How to proper trim dog's nails

Use our simple guide to take care of your dog's nails quickly and safely.

1. Prepare your supplies in advance

Before you begin, prepare all the materials you will be using and make sure you have them on hand.

• Dog nail clippers or files

There are many different tools for grooming dog nails, but they all fall into one of three types:

- Dog nail clippers are the most common tools for trimming dog nails. They are effective and available with different characteristics and in different models (in the shape of pliers or scissors, with an ergonomic or rubber-coated grip, with protection).

- the guillotine clippers have a single blade that cuts off the excess nail. They're easier to use than the other options, but aren't quite as robust; they are generally suitable for small dogs with finer nails.

- nail files usually have a small rotating disc which files the tips of the dog's nails as it rotates.

• Hemostatic powder

It is useful to have this powder on hand if you accidentally incise the living flesh (dermis) during the operation. Simply dip the affected area in a bowl containing the powder to quickly stop the bleeding.

• Awards

Keep treats or snacks your dog loves on hand to help him get through this difficult time, especially the first few times he trims his nails.

2. Start with the dog's front legs

Start at the forelimbs by gently but firmly holding one leg still and decide exactly where to start cutting.

A good tip: to trim the nails of the dog's hind legs, have your four-legged friend lie on its side; this will facilitate access to the hind legs and the grip during the cutting operation.

3. Trim nails, avoiding raw flesh

Always cut the tip of the nails from top to bottom, with a cut perpendicular to the nail. Avoid cutting them at a different angle.

Remember that the base of your dog's nails is raw flesh (dermis) and contains nerve endings and blood vessels. You must do everything possible to avoid clipping this area so as not to draw blood from the dog's nails, which will otherwise be painful. If your dog has whitish nails, you should easily spot the line where the soft pink of raw flesh begins. Try to leave 2 mm of space from the raw meat to be safe. If your dog has dark nails, unfortunately you won't be able to see where the raw flesh begins. However, when you start cutting you should be able to see a darker spot in the center of the nail where the raw flesh is.

If you accidentally cut raw flesh, don't panic! An overreaction on your part would lead the dog to think that the situation is more serious than it really is. This would create a negative association in the animal with nail trimming. So don't make a big deal of it: just apply the styptic powder to the affected area until it stops bleeding and then give your dog a treat and a few words of comfort.

When in doubt, it's always better to cut too little rather than too much: you can always continue in small steps. If your dog has dark nails or if you don't feel like it, take him to a professional groomer or vet.

4. When you're done, reward your dog with treats and treats

You will need to trim your dog's nails regularly, so make sure it's a positive experience. When you're done, reward him with his favorite food and praise him for his good behavior.

Grooming

Grooming, contrary to what many think, is a really important issue, which underlies the health and well-being of our friend. This term does not mean only the bath and the care of the dog's fur, but its hygiene in the total sense.

The dog must be groomed not only for purely aesthetic reasons, but for health and well-being reasons too: it's a way to shape and protects our dog from the risk of infections or parasites.

Method and frequency of treatment depends on the breed and type of hair: the longer it is, the more obviously it needs frequent care.

On average, a grooming every 30-40 days is the general rule.

As specified from the beginning, grooming is a matter of hygiene and health, and therefore there are some treatments that must never be overlooked as they concern aspects relating to the well-being of the dog. We are talking about:

✓ Bath
✓ Nail trimming
✓ Ear cleaning
✓ Hair shaving
✓ Eye cleaning
✓ Elimination of any knots from the hair
✓ Personal care

We have already talked about many of these above. In this subsection we will talk about the elements that have not yet been explored in depth.

Grooming: hair cutting

There are 3 main techniques:
✓ Shearing
✓ Scissor cut
✓ Stripping

The first reason to consider when choosing the most suitable technique is the breed of dog and the type of coat (long or short, curly or smooth, soft or hard). In a second step it is also necessary to evaluate the purpose of the cut, exactly as for us humans: a comfortable cut for every day will in fact be very different from a hairstyle that we want to show during an important event which in our case can be a ceremony while for our four-legged friend can be a beauty contest or a skill competition.

The most particular technique is that of stripping, which is carried out with a special knife without blades. Applicable only to certain breeds, characterized by a rough or bristly coat, it requires considerable experience and skill on the part of those who perform it.

Personal hygiene of the dog

This may be a touchy subject, but your pet also needs regular genital care.

Long-haired dogs, for example, can experience very strong discomfort if foreign bodies such as hair or other waste block the body orifices. Taking care of your dog also means this: the more diligent you are in cleaning the tail and the genital region, the less likely your pet will develop infections or other types of pathologies. What are the risks they could incur and how do you take care of such a delicate area as that of the genitals?

Let's begin by analyzing the risks associated with poor or lack of maintenance of its tail.

Don't be afraid, just get familiar with your pet's body. Know that you can help him relieve his pain or other discomfort.

The tail area is a real hot spot because it can be prone to injury.

It is therefore essential to check it regularly, especially at the base.

In many cases dogs show that they have a very thick and matted coat right at the tail, which can make it difficult to brush. However, it is necessary, especially if your pet likes to roll around in the garden: it is precisely outdoors, especially on the street, that dirt and other materials could take root in the hair.

To comb it you can help yourself with a detangling spray. Use great caution, especially if you have to cut some portions of hair.

It is recommended to trim especially around the anus area, to prevent bodily waste from adhering to the skin or coat. Some dogs obviously don't need this arrangement, while others appear more messy, due to their type of coat.

As for the genital and anal area, know that the sexual organs of dogs are very sensitive, so it is important that you pay close attention and that you manage the situation with great caution.

For both the genital and anal areas, it is recommended to cut the portions of hair that could block the orifices.

In many cases, urine could affect long fringes of hair and contribute to skin rashes and infections, especially if the area comes into contact with foreign bodies and dirt.

For male dogs it is sufficient to trim one centimeter around the penile area, for female dogs the hair must be shortened in the area around the vulva.

Female dogs, in particular, experience genital discharge that could make the vulva area sticky.

It is therefore necessary to maintain hygiene by freeing the tract from excess hair, especially if its fur is very thick.

Cleaning the dog's anal genital area

You could help yourself with a blade but be extremely careful as even a small injury could cause your bitch great pain, as well as a serious risk of infection.

After shaving it is recommended, if possible, to bathe her and let her rest in warm water: this solution could calm her down, considering that the reason for the losses is probably of an infectious nature.

The anal glands, on the other hand, can cause quite a few problems in dogs.

Trimming or clipping the fur can help keep this area clean. But be careful: this could be an extremely smelly procedure. It is therefore recommended to use rubber gloves and clean the area with a damp cloth or baby wipe.

If your pet has difficulty or is uncomfortable being touched, ask your veterinarian for help.

We have also finished doing an all-round analysis of our dog's hygiene and cleanliness. In the second chapter of this fifth guide, however, we will focus on the health of our 4-legged friend.

Chapter 2: Health and Wellness

Keeping your dog healthy is crucial for their well-being. This chapter covers recognizing signs of illness or injury in your dog, preventative care (such as vaccinations, heartworm prevention), and senior dog care and addressing age-related health issues.

Recognizing signs of illness or injury in your dog

Usually, the dog in our life is happy and healthy, free from any problems.

Sometimes, however, like us, the dog gets sick.

It is important to understand the possible problems, so that you know how to manage them and whether to take your dog to the vet.

Here are six health problems your dog can most commonly experience and some ways you can help your four-legged friend overcome them.

1. The first of these is diarrhea. It can be caused by viruses such as parvo virus, parasites or food problems. If you see anything resembling blood in your dog's stool, you should bring your pet to the vet immediately. Alternatively, monitor his condition and make sure he has enough water to not become dehydrated. If the food you are feeding your dog is one of the cheaper ones, it is likely that he has ingested some corn or wheat gluten to which he is allergic. Try switching to a higher quality dog food and see if that helps him feel better.

2. The second problem is fleas. Fleas can spread quickly and cover your dog's body with pesky biting insects. It is easy to get fleas from other animals or when staying in an area where they are numerous. You will find your dog biting on one area or scratching excessively. Both of these reactions can tear the skin and lead to secondary infections, so it's important to treat fleas promptly. In your dog's bed you may find something like salt and pepper, which are the larvae and dirt of fleas. Failure to treat fleas can lead to tapeworms, blood loss, or infection.

3. Worms can be transmitted not only by fleas. You can also get them from other infected dogs or contaminated soil at dog parks. Tapeworms, roundworms, heartworm immitis and other parasites are not only irritating but can be fatal, especially for puppies and older dogs. Worms on the outside of the animal can cause dry patches or skin irritation, or they can

127

appear in the feces in a rice grain-like form. You may find your dog dragging himself on the ground due to parasite irritated backsides. A change in appetite or significant weight loss can also be a sign. See your vet about worming – you will need deworming treatment from your vet.

4. Ear infections are also a common problem. Numerous factors could represent the main causes, such as mites and bacteria or fungal infections and allergies. A good diet of high-quality dog food can help keep allergies under control and even reduce the likelihood of developing fungal infections. However, you may also need to use ear drops to treat the infection. How do you know if your dog has an infection? You may see your dog shaking his head or scratching his ear all the time. Severe infections can cause problems with balance, as the infection affects the inside, or generate a strong odor. Redness or swelling on their ear is another signal.

Recognize the signs of injury in your dog

The behaviors that can be used to evaluate pain and therefore a possible injury are different. Here we will look at the main ones:

1. Observe vitality and mobility:

   ✓ Observe the level of energy and attention,
   ✓ The fluidity of the most common movements such as sitting, lying down, transitions from one position to another.
   ✓ While taking the stairs
   ✓ Jump
   ✓ Change direction
   ✓ Use the litter box (for cats)

2. Mood and Temperament.
   ✓ Anxiety
   ✓ Sadness
   ✓ Depression
   ✓ Be reserved and introverted

- ✓ Unable to relate
- ✓ Are synonymous with malaise.

In the opposite sense, however, a pain-free dog will be playful, outgoing, confident in his movements and in his relationship with others.

Aggressive behaviors such as growling and biting, especially in relation to attempts to physically approach the dog, can also be considered pain signals.

If you try to pick him up, or caress him in sore spots, he may react by turning over (or even just looking more intensely at the part you're touching)

3. Also observe the reaction of the skin only.

Sometimes, if one-part hurts, the dog curls up the skin, moves it under the fingers, as if to recoil from the touch.

- ✓ Depression in dogs
- ✓ Loss of muscle mass
- ✓ Postural changes
- ✓ Sleep more than usual
- ✓ Hind limbs weak

4. Self-care.

Decreased ability to feed and drink can also be a sign of pain.

- ✓ Can you reach the bowl?
- ✓ Can you stand the entire time you eat or drink?
- ✓ Does it clean?
- ✓ Excessive self-licking is a typical sign of pain, especially in cats, which show their discomfort just like that.
- ✓ the ease or otherwise in maintaining the position during the needs.
- ✓ Rest: Can you sit still, or do you do it too often?

Both walking incessantly without finding peace and the increase in hours of sleep are to be interpreted as signs of discomfort.

These are the signs of pain you need to see and observe in your dog.

- ✓ Lameness,
- ✓ Impaired gait,

✓ Stiffness in movement,

✓ Postural changes,

✓ Difficulty walking on slippery surfaces such as ceramic or parquet floors,

✓ Reluctance to get into the car, onto the sofa.

All these data, methodically collected by you and your trusted veterinarian, will form a diary for chronic pain assessment and its monitoring over time.

Preventative care

Now let's see what the preventive measures that can promote the health and longevity of our beloved dog are.

Routine dog health checkups

If you have a dog you will have, at least once, experienced a feeling of difficulty and helplessness in fully understanding his state of health. Our animal friends are able to tell us when something is wrong, and this is why you too will have happened to run urgently to the vet without however having clear the origin of the discomfort.

Often when dogs show signs of pain or discomfort they do so when the problem is already there, and we find ourselves fearful that they will suffer.

With a series of routine exams to be divided over the year, it is possible to keep the health of your dog under control. These are mostly non-invasive tests that will not cause discomfort to the animal and which, at the same time, will allow you to have a complete picture of its health. Here are the best routine dog health checkups to do on a regular basis:

Veterinary cancer prevention check-up

Dog tumors can be dangerous because they are too often discovered late. An annual visit that includes in-depth blood tests and ultrasounds such as those of the abdomen and chest are a tool of great help for an early cancer diagnosis.

Leishmaniasis, a vaccine to avoid taking risks

With Leishmania, we mean an infectious and contagious disease whose cause is a small parasite. It causes deep skin lesions, ulcerations, fever and lethargy. It is a potentially very dangerous disease that can be discovered in advance through a serological investigation and can be prevented with an annual vaccination.

Vaccination for filariasis

The disease is caused by a mosquito bite and can manifest itself in different ways. In its most serious form, it will lead the dog to have heart and lung problems which will only show up when the state of the disease is advanced. It is therefore essential to prevent filariasis by performing a vaccination.

Dermatological check-up

Sometimes it can be difficult to check the health of the dog's skin, especially for long-haired coats. Irritations or dermatitis can be a cause of annoyance for the animal which can lead it to scratch itself insistently and sometimes to injure itself. Dog dermatological problems are often transient and solvable (for example with a change of diet) but sometimes they can hide other pathologies. It is at this point essential to ask your veterinarian to inspect your dog's skin during a checkup.

Beware of common diseases

Your dog may be suffering from a tummy ache or dry, flaky skin at some point in his life – these are both common health conditions and a visit to your vet should put you at ease. Sometimes, a gradual change to your meal plan can make a positive difference. Large dog breeds are prone to specific health problems, such as arthritis in later life.

Prevent accidents

Unfortunately, even dogs can have unexpected accidents. So, you should avoid "ticks" (a nasty pest that often resides in tall grass).

Avoid any and eye damage too from spiky plants. If your dog meets ticks, never try to deal with them yourself – they're tough stuff to remove and are best dealt with by your vet. To prevent your small dog from choking, you can give him food that is small enough to chew and swallow easily and play fetch with a ball instead of a stick.

Food plan

A correct and correct diet of the dog is the basis of daily well-being. It's not just about choosing a food you like but using one that fits your characteristics and habits that can change over time. Conditions such as a sedentary lifestyle, changes in the rhythms of life, the alternation of the seasons can lead our dog to have different needs. It is therefore good not to take his diet for granted and to study a food plan for his well-being.

Annual vaccinations against rabies and major diseases

The annual vaccinations of the dog are essential and allow to protect it from diseases such as distemper, leptospirosis, infectious hepatitis, parvovirus, rabies, babesiosis, borreliosis and infectious tracheobronchitis. These are potentially very dangerous and contagious diseases against which it is good to protect the dog.

Orthopedic veterinary visit

For particular breeds or in certain age groups (specifically youth and seniority) orthopedic checks can be very important. Skeletal health is essential for the well-being of the dog and through a veterinary comparison it is possible to evaluate the need or not for specialized radiographic investigations.

Ear check

Dog ear health should not be underestimated. A periodic check performed by a veterinarian will allow you to understand if there are problems such as infections or parasites. It will also help you understand how to perform a thorough home cleaning of your dog's ears in order to prevent any diseases.

Deworming

Worms and dog parasites are a rather common problem, but that should not be underestimated. Deworming is the only effective cure for eradicating an infestation which in most cases affects the dog's intestine, undermining its health. You don't have to fear anything, because it is a safe and non-invasive procedure, which involves the oral administration of a dewormer for dogs for a certain period of time (usually a few days), possibly to be repeated cyclically (depending on the vet's instructions). When is it good to deworm a puppy instead? Usually, the first deworming of the dog should be done within the first month of life with reminders every two weeks or months depending on the indications of the veterinarian. This period usually coincides with weaning, a phase in which the puppy's immune defenses are lowered, therefore it is very important to prevent the most serious side effects that an infestation of worms can give. Please note: if the puppy is infected, the mother will most likely be infected too, so it is advisable to extend the antiworm prophylaxis to the bitch as well.

Healthy ways to exercise

While it's tempting to pick up and carry your small dog if you're in a hurry, helping them stay active at all ages is an important rule of thumb for dog health. Regular exercise will boost your dog's energy levels, keep his weight stable, and maintain a healthy heart and strong immune system. Vary up your routine by walking at different times of the day and visiting different places.

Young small dogs will also enjoy walking on soft surfaces like grass and sand until their paws have hardened.

Remember not to overdo it, though, and try not to exercise your dog right after a meal.

Teeth and oral hygiene

Too often the health of the dog's teeth is neglected. It would be good to gently brush our four-legged friend's teeth to facilitate the removal of food residues that can cause tartar and subsequently infections.

Some dogs are particularly prone to it; therefore, it is advisable to periodically visit them and possibly plan scaling.

Blood tests

Blood is the mirror of many pathologies, from small problems to more important ones.

Periodically performing blood tests on your dog will allow you to have a more defined picture of his health in a non-invasive and effective way.

Cardiological check-up in the dog

An echocardiographic examination allows you to study the morphology of the animal's heart and to investigate the presence or absence of pathologies.

This is a recommended preventative test for certain breeds that are prone to cardiac abnormalities either from birth or by acquisition. The examination may include early identification of problems which, if not discovered in time, can be very dangerous.

Sterilization

We have left this topic for last not because it is less important but because of the particular delicacy of the topic. Choosing to neuter your dog can sometimes be a cause of difficulty.

However, it is essential to discuss with the vet to understand what the best choice for your dog's health might be, always remembering that we must not project ourselves into him but think only and exclusively of his well-being.

Planning a series of routine dog health visits specific to his age and characteristics is the greatest gift you can give yourself.

Your four-legged friend will improve in health, and you will be more serene and confident that you are doing the best for his well-being.

Senior dog care and addressing age-related health issues

The dog like man undergoes aging, but unlike us it has a shorter average life of about 13 to a maximum of 20 years, depending on the breed and lifestyle. Here we describe the various pathologies that our dogs can encounter as they age. Some are very similar to those that can come to us men in old age too.

There are small tricks to make the dog live with serenity and make him face this stage of life in a less painful way if affected by pathologies of a certain type. Some diseases tend to be part of the aging of all dogs, others manifest themselves as typical of certain breeds and are pathologies closely linked to the physicality of the dog, to its size.

Our beloved 4-legged friends today boast more attention and even the treatments available have improved and are constantly evolving, so don't worry, even the aging of the dog can be lived in a more serene way.

Health of the senior dog: here are the pathologies

Our beloved dogs have an average lifespan of 10 to 13 years, very limited compared to that of us men: to have a more precise estimate we must not forget that their life expectancy is also determined by the size that the dog will reach as an adult.

The small sizes range from 15 to 18 years, the medium ones from 12 to 14 years and the large ones from 9 to 11 years. What can I say, seven of our years could be equivalent to a year of our dog's life. Already from the age of 7 upwards we can begin to classify dogs in a seniority phase, but this depends a lot on the breed, size and lifestyle that the dog has led.

Aging is obviously not only a physical factor but also a cognitive one, which compromises the functions of memory and learning. Senile aging in dogs can manifest itself with difficulty in recognizing family members, a disorientation that recurs even when they move and find themselves in places they don't recognize, to such an extent that when they are lost, they have difficulty even returning home. He obeys his master less, plays little and can also disrupt sleep and wake cycles by staying awake at night and sleeping during the day.

As in humans, dog aging is also characterized by some signs, for example white hair on the muzzle, reduced hearing, slower movements and reflexes followed obviously by a tendency to be less lively and the need to rest longer. long. Cataract problems and decreased vision can occur.

Even chewing becomes more difficult, it can be characterized by the loss of a few teeth. The metabolism slows down, the digestive system works less, the energy requirement is also reduced. This can lead to obesity and consequently generate heart and lung problems, so it is important to pay attention to nutrition and find out about the most suitable food for senior dogs.

Incontinence is another problem that can be found in an elderly dog, it can be due to organic dysfunctions but also to confusional disorientations where, for example, it does not recognize the carpet from the grass. The elderly dog becomes weaker and exposed to diseases, which can be prevented with the appropriate vaccinations. Arthritis, tumors, heart problems, kidney disorders are other problems that can occur in a dog's advanced age.

To prevent some of these diseases it is important to have your dog visit the vet and take some small precautions such as making him follow an adequate diet.

Aging can also lead to some diseases such as Cushing's disease in dogs, it is caused by an overproduction of cortisol, hypothyroidism is due to the malfunctioning of the thyroid gland: with the right medicines the symptoms of these diseases can be alleviated. Diabetes is another widespread disease in dogs, it obviously involves a regulation of nutrition, and it may be necessary to make insulin.

In the list I indicate some actions that we can do to keep our dog in shape:

- ✓ Regular checkups at the vet after a certain age
- ✓ Follow a proper diet
- ✓ Don't let the dog lack physical movement
- ✓ Teeth care

These small tricks can help our dog to live his old age with greater serenity. Today more attention is paid to one's pets, treatments have also evolved in the veterinary sector, there are specific anti-inflammatories for elderly dogs and also elderly dog supplements that allow our beloved 4-legged friends to live better.

Alternative healing methods can be adopted such as small tricks and more holistic therapies linked to natural methods in addition to the classic pharmacological solutions.

Let us always remember one important thing before concluding this chapter: an elderly dog is not synonymous with a sick dog. However, it must be treated and respected, considered as an animal still capable of doing many things including that of continuing to play, because the best vitamins for older dogs are the care and affection, we give them every day.

Apart from this, surely a visit to your vet will also be able to shed light on the possibility of administering tonics to your dog to "confuse" with food.

In the last book of this guide, we will deal with mental health as well as the third book, but this time from a behavioral point of view.

PART 6: MENTAL HEALTHY FOR DOG

Introduction

We conclude our training bible with this sixth guide that strictly concerns the mental health of our dog. Specifically, we will talk about both possible behavioral problems and some targeted advice when it comes to traveling with your dog. With this information you will have the complete picture on how to behave in any situation and from any point of view, with your beloved dog.

Chapter 1: Dealing with Common Behavior Problems

Even well-trained dogs may develop behavior problems. This chapter covers separation anxiety, resource guarding, and fear and aggression towards other dogs or people.

Separation anxiety

Moving away from your pet is never an easy choice and it can prove even more difficult for your dog. In fact, living with a dog means having a real shadow that follows you at all times of the day. During 2020 each of us had to change our habits and with us also our pets. The recent period of restrictions has in fact accustomed our dogs to always being in the company of someone, to then bring them back dramatically to normal, with whole days of solitude during our working hours. All this has led to more and more cases of anxiety in dogs. But specifically, what is separation anxiety? Separation anxiety is the dog's response to discomfort felt when left alone. As we said in the introduction to this chapter, it is something that can affect any dog, even the most trained one. It is a problem that causes stress and feelings of guilt even in the owner, but separation anxiety in dogs derives from his herd animal instinct and therefore from the need to live in a group feeling strength and protection. Therefore, being alone can lead to emotional problems that can translate into behavioral problems.

Separation anxiety: the symptoms

None of our four-legged friends like to be alone and not have anyone to show their love to, but some are particularly sensitive to this situation, showing real nervous reactions that take the form of destroyed sofas and furniture, floor, constant barking, or socks all over the house.

It should be noted that dogs do not perform these behaviors out of spite, but it is their way of reacting to being terrified. Separation anxiety is a very frequent behavioral issue: one in seven dogs suffers from separation anxiety. It is estimated that 13 to 18% of dogs show signs of being unwell under these circumstances. Depending on the individual dog and the severity of his separation anxiety, symptoms and related behaviors can range from mild to extreme.

A study found that the most common behaviors related to separation anxiety are: destroying the house (displayed by 71% of dogs), excessive barking (in 61% of dogs) and excessive defecation (reported in 28% of subjects).

Mild symptoms occur when dogs are panting or crying, pacing constantly, licking themselves excessively, tending to follow their owners around the house, and are unable to settle into their beds.

The most serious behaviors occur when the dog paws or bites the bed, drools, destroys the house, furniture and tries to escape. Other symptoms to watch out for: Doesn't eat or drink, runs around the house without finding peace of mind, licks and nibbles causing injuries, shows aggressive behaviors, vomiting and diarrhea, tachycardia.

Separation anxiety: the causes

It is not possible to generalize and state what exactly triggers separation anxiety in dogs but there are a few factors that have been identified as potential triggers. Among the various causes can be included cases of reintegration into a different family, death or prolonged absence of a family member or other traumatic events, but also a genetic predisposition. Dogs with difficult situations behind them are more sensitive to separation from the reference person.

5 ways to reduce separation anxiety

Here you are five functional ways to manage your dog separation anxiety:

1. Gradually prepare your dog for separation

Introduce the new step-by-step routine and get him used to being alone for some time each day. Start letting him know your upcoming times and plans, so it will be easier for him to understand the reason for your absence at certain times of the day. Also, he tries not to get all the members of the house out at once but to do it one at a time.

2. Identify your anxiety triggers

If your dog starts to fidget when you take your keys, put on your shoes or a jacket and you perceive that these are the factors that generate anxiety in your dog, change your routine or try to do it without involving him.

3.Practice reinforcement activities

Develop positive associations with your departure by giving him a snack or baby food before going out and put his favorite toys in the kennel. It can also help to leave the television or radio on – these sounds will help block out neighborhood noise that could lead to your dog barking. These little instruments can also help him relax as they represent the everyday sounds your dog is used to hearing even when you are in the house and can simulate the presence of someone.

4.Limit parties on your return

Don't give too much importance to your departure or your return home. Don't give him an intense cuddle time before you leave or act like he hasn't seen you in years when you get back (wait until he calms down before giving him attention when you get home). The goal is to make it clear that the detachment and the return of the master are simply daily activities.

5. Get him used to independence even in your presence

One way to limit separation anxiety is to train your dog to be independent even during times when you are in the same place. Getting the dog used to being with us 24 hours a day and always being available for him makes him dependent on this condition. In fact, when there are sudden changes in habits, he immediately feels in danger and manifests his malaise. Place his toys in the room where he will be in your absence.

Remember that nobody likes to be left alone for long periods of time.

Resource guarding

Resource guarding in dogs is a behavior that animals develop to protect or hide something they consider important, and fear might disappear.

The guarding of resources in dogs is one of the issues that most concern owners. Hence, we have decided to devote an entire paragraph to this behavioral anomaly. Not only will we explain to you what it is, but we will also give you some suggestions to fix it or limit resource guarding in dogs.

Returning to the question of what the resource guarding is, in general this obsessive attention falls on food, toys or even the doghouse. But it can occur with many other objects or in different situations. To protect their assets, dogs usually growl, bark or use their body muscles.

In extreme cases, dogs can bite the air and even their owner.

The main problem of resource protection in dogs concerns the timing of intervention. If this behavioral anomaly is not addressed early, there is a risk of worsening the animal's psychological health picture. Obviously, all animals have a reluctance to share what is theirs. But if this becomes an obsession, coexistence itself suffers, given that the dog stops playing, eating and living normally. There are many possible causes for a dog to start guarding its assets.

This problem does not necessarily concern only stray dogs or dogs with a stormy past behind them.

Alongside these episodes of abuse, violence and trauma, there is also room for spoiled dogs to which, from the very first months of life, practically everything has been allowed and allowed.

Despite this, in general, we can say that there is a greater prevalence of this behavior in dogs that are insecure, that have little trust in their human family or that are very stressed.

However, when looking for resource guarding solutions in dogs, the cause doesn't matter – you are looking for solutions for the present behavior.

Since every case is different, some dogs pass resource guarding easily while others require more time and patience.

As with any behavioral problem, choosing a dog trainer who practices positive training, and family involvement, is critical to achieving stable and definitive results.

Examples of resource guarding in dogs

The typical example, which usually illustrates resource guarding in dogs, is when the animal growls and does not allow anyone near its food bowl. He can do it with all humans, in front of the owner or if he is close to other animals. So, this is not a selective attitude.

It is also considered, as protection of resources, the attitude of the dog that does not allow other animals to approach its owner.

An act of extreme jealousy, no doubt. But even a place, an area of the house, can become a "resource" to protect. For example, the kennel or even a sofa, an armchair, a carpet.

Anyway, it's vital to understand that dogs don't growl just because of resource protection. For example, if your dog lets you use the couch but only growls when he's asleep and you wake him up, that's just a response to annoying behavior.

Tips and remedies

The possible solutions to the resource guarding anomaly in dogs are different depending on the case.

Finding the root of the problem and solving it is a job that can only be done successfully by a specialized dog trainer.

It is important that you adopt positive, non-blaming, and dominance-based therapy, as this may only make the situation worse.

It is necessary to contact an expert educator, but there are also other measures that can be implemented at home.

Since we know that insecurity about losing a valuable resource often causes this behavior, you can allow your dog to enjoy this resource without limits.

That is, if the dog guards the food, it would be a good idea to let the food be always available.

If the animal gets stressed when you touch "his" bowls, you could wash and fill them, for example when the dog is sleeping or away from home: that is, when he doesn't see you.

Likewise, if he protects his bed, avoid moving it or disturbing him when he rests.

Usually, trying to forcefully demonstrate who is "ruling" is often a very bad idea: at best, it will exacerbate the problem. Worst-case scenario, you'll get a well-deserved bite.

Resource management in the puppy: avoiding behavioral problems

If your dog is a puppy and hasn't yet shown signs of poor resource management, you can prevent the problem from appearing by following some basic tips. Train him and teach him the basic commands for dropping items and ignoring things. Both exercises help him to have self-control, thus reducing impulsive reactions towards resources such as games or food and understanding that managing what he has correctly leads him to something positive (rewards such as prizes, cuddles, etc.).

1. Don't let your dog be possessive with toys.

To avoid mismanagement of the dog's resources, the ideal is to work with him and teach him to release objects. Picking up and returning objects must be a stimulating and fun activity, but it is very important that the animal does not feel that the toy has been snatched from its mouth or suddenly taken away from it.

2. Avoid your dog being possessive of people.

It is undoubtedly the most important aspect of resource management. It is not good for the dog to consider you or another person something to be defended because it can lead to serious aggression problems. It is for this reason that socialization from a young age is very important. In this process, objects, animals, people and environments are presented to the dog and it is essential that he meets people of all kinds (adults, children, etc.) letting himself be petted and interacting in a positive way. Remember to reward positive behaviors by following the rules of positive reinforcement.

If this phase is done correctly, the dog will not have resource management problems with people because he will understand that they are not dangerous for him or for you.

3. Don't let your dog be possessive about food.

Avoiding this problem is relatively easy. You'll want to start giving bits of dog food directly from your hand to the puppy to reward him during training or when he behaves properly.

Then you will need to feed him from your hand before putting the food into the bowl making sure he sees that you are feeding him: this way the dog will have to understand that you are feeding him and that he does not have to protect the bowl while eating.

Once you see that he completely trusts you, you can even put your hand close to the bowl while he's eating. Especially if it's a puppy or if it's an animal that has never had problems related to aggression or possessiveness, there shouldn't be any problems. Don't feed him when he's aggressive, or you'll reinforce the behavior. Have him calm down and wait for the situation to return to normal.

If there are no problems following these tips, continue this program until your dog is an adult by occasionally feeding him directly from your hand. Have the rest of the family or people who come to your house often do this too so that the dog gets used to other people too.

Remember to use these tips only with puppies and not if there are resource management issues in the dog. We advise you, for this kind of situations, to contact a professional.

Fear and aggression towards other dogs or people

The dog who is afraid of people is an animal that can fear different types of human beings, for different reasons.

Sometimes it can happen that it is not men who are afraid of four-legged friends, but that it is the dog who is afraid of people. In fact, there are different circumstances and situations that can frighten and disturb the peace of the animal: there are dogs that are afraid of people in general, others that are afraid of children, still others that fear men who have dark clothes, etc. In any case, however, to help your four-legged friend overcome this fear, you can either contact a specialized educator or perform a series of actions that can reassure the dog. But why is the dog afraid of people? And how to help him overcome this malaise?

Usually, we hear about the fear of dogs, also called cynophobia, and not about dogs being afraid of people. However, the behavior of the dog that is afraid is a state of mind that is already found in the first stages of socialization of the puppy. Precisely when the animal is in this age group it

143

is essential to educate it and get it used to the presence not only of its peers, but also of people, objects and environments that will then become part of its daily life once it becomes an adult. If this is not the case, fears and phobias arise and feed on the dog.

Generally, the main reason why the dog is afraid of people is due to the poor socialization he has been used to. However, there are also other causes for which this fear can be triggered in the four-legged friend:

✓ Lack of constant contact with people
✓ Traumatic experiences related to the presence of people
✓ Genetic causes, as in the case in which the dog is the child of parents who are by nature fearful
✓ Use of punishment as a method of education and teaching
✓ Contact with a few people other than the usual ones during the life of the animal
✓ Aging, i.e., often the appearance of cognitive dysfunction syndrome
✓ Use of violence or scolding to give commands to the dog.

A dog who is fearful of people will tend to act differently when confronted with them than a dog who has a phobia. The fearful dog will try to flee, move, or stand still or attack, while a phobic dog may have an uncontrolled reaction and be attacked by panic attacks.

How to help a dog who is afraid of people?

To help a dog who is afraid of people, the fundamental thing is to always be able to maintain calm and tranquility. In fact, the four-legged friend takes the owner as an example and a model to follow, so it is good to remain relaxed and peaceful to try to improve the dog's behavior. The first thing that needs to be done is therefore to win the dog's trust, making him perceive that the human pack leader is a balanced and serene person, able to defend him from what represents a threat to him. To help a dog who is afraid of people, you need to distract him from what scares him. The best method in this sense is the game: it is in fact possible through this means to be able to induce the animal to get closer and closer to what inspires fear.

If, for example, the dog is afraid of children, it can be brought in the presence of some small humans, ordering it to stand still and not approach. The dog can then be distracted by playing together, waving the toy in front of it and having the four-legged friend follow him who will try to catch it. By doing so, you will be able to get closer and closer to the child, and perhaps the dog will not notice his presence until he is a few centimeters away from him. He might still get scared, but still he will understand that nothing bad happened to him even though he got so close to what he feared. Through these behaviors it will be possible to help a dog who is afraid of people because little by little it will be possible to desensitize him, until the fright reactions disappear.

Dogs who are afraid of other dogs: what to do?

Walking around with a dog who is fearful of other dogs can lead to unpleasant situations. Follow these tips to learn how to handle this emotion appropriately. Before talking about suggestions, know that dogs express themselves through body language, with facial expressions, body posture and position of the tail, which indicate their emotions.

A frightened dog:

- ✓ His ears are folded back or close to his head.
- ✓ Muscle tension. The animal may even start shaking.
- ✓ Tends to curl up the body.
- ✓ It has a low tail, sometimes between the legs.
- ✓ Start barking and panting.
- ✓ Try to get away from what scares him.

As fear increases, the animal may defecate, urinate or even make repetitive (stereotyped) movements due to the stress generated by the situation. Some, on the other hand, react with excessive calm or sleepiness.

But why are dogs afraid of other dogs?

Dogs who are fearful of other dogs usually have a motivation. The most frequent causes are:

- ✓ Lack of socialization. The socialization phase is essential in the puppy's life to avoid phobias during the adult phase. This period goes from the first three weeks of life up to three months. In this period, it is essential to provide the puppy with as many stimuli as possible: only in this way will he learn to recognize another of his species, which are his friends, will he learn not to bite and to express himself through body language, among other things.

- ✓ Previous traumatic experience. A previous negative experience with another dog may be enough to make the animal fear another of its kind.
- ✓ Behavior reinforced by the owner. Dogs easily recognize the emotions of their owners and if you are tense and afraid when you approach other dogs, you will transmit that feeling to your pet, for example by squeezing the leash.

As for the suggestions, know that preventing your dog from being afraid of other dogs is not an easy task: it will take time and effort. You can't force him to interact with others, but you can gradually reduce his fear of meeting other dogs walking on the street by following a number of guidelines during walks:

- ✓ Lower the voltage. It is advisable to use a long leash, about three meters long, to guarantee the animal more peaceful walks without tension or leash jerks when it crosses another dog. That way, he won't associate the walk with feeling scared.
- ✓ Generate a habit. Keep a certain distance from other dogs that the animal feels comfortable with. The owner must show a calm demeanor and always use positive reinforcement in these situations. Over time, this distance may be reduced.
- ✓ Observe the animal closely. It is very important to pay attention to the animal's body language to study its limits and recognize its progress.

By training them this way, their fear of other dogs will gradually disappear and little by little they will be able to start interacting with strangers.

With these tips on how to manage dogs' fear of other similar dogs, our first chapter is over. In the next and last one, we will deal with managing the "travel" situation with your four-legged friend.

Chapter 2: Traveling with Your Dog

Many dog owners like to travel with their furry friends. This chapter covers planning for trips with your dog, safety considerations for car travel, and finding dog-friendly accommodations and activities.

Planning for trips with your dog

Nowadays, the dog – as well as any other pet – is considered to all intents and purposes a member of the family. If before we were forced to leave our beloved animal in the care of a dog sitter, today even this extra expense is completely out of date because, with a little planning, you can share most of your travel adventures with your furry friends, at home but also abroad. Here is a brief guide on how to plan a trip with your dog based on the vehicle chosen.

Traveling with the dog by plane

While rules vary from airline to airline, your dog is generally only allowed to fly in the cabin if it's small enough to fit in a kennel under the seat in front of you. Larger sizes, or over 10 kg, impose the obligation to travel in the hold, with baggage and cargo.

Traveling with the dog by car

If you plan on taking a long car ride with your dog, you'll need to anticipate his needs along the way. There are many safety measures and products that can help you to have a healthy trip with your dog safely in the car. It is important that you choose a suitable and comfortable solution for your pet and that the system is correctly installed and secured in the vehicle. We will talk about it in the next paragraph.

Traveling with the dog on a motorcycle

Not all dogs are comfortable traveling by motorcycle, plus you'll need to think about all the additional equipment needed to keep your pet safe during the journey, no matter how long or short. However, if you're ready to take your dog on a new adventure, here's everything you need to know to always keep them safe.

Traveling with the dog by ship

Except for assistance dogs, pets are only welcome on a few cruise lines and vaccination certificates are always required. Some lines welcome dogs on board in private cabins, but most limit pets to limited areas. Contact your cruise line ahead of time to find out their policies and which of their ships have a dog kennel area.

Traveling with the dog by train

Our four-legged friends are welcome in first and second class of any train category. Some smaller trains may restrict carriage to only small dogs while others, such as the Eurostar, only allow access to guide dogs. In any case, our dog must be kept in a special carrier, so as not to cause damage to people and things.

Safety considerations for car travel

Traveling with your dog by car is an experience that all Pet parents should have: the sense of freedom and our puppy's ears fluttering out the window are a priceless joy, whatever your destination!

When it comes to bringing a dog in the car, however, everyone's safety must always come first. There are precise rules for transporting dogs by car.

Here are all the guidelines for traveling by car with our four-legged friend, with particular attention to what the law requires and what accessories are needed for a safe and worry-free journey with your best friend!

The law provides that one or more dogs can be brought in the car as long as they do not annoy the driver and do not constitute a possible source of distraction.

For this reason, pets must be kept in a special carrier or in the compartment behind the driving area, specially divided by a net or other suitable means.

Where can the dog stay in the car

The alternatives that the law provides for the transport of dogs by car are of two types:

1. The dog can travel by car if kept in a special kennel or similar accessories
2. Otherwise, if you are not equipped with a kennel, the dog should still be kept separate from the driver by means of a dividing net or other suitable means (e.g., seat belts).

Among the permitted accessories, the pet carrier is certainly the most common and the simplest to use. It is an accessory that keeps the dog safe and at the same time limits its movements, so that you can drive in complete peace of mind and safety.

On the market there are different types of carriers that are used above all for small or medium-sized dogs. Pets appreciate carriers or kennels that are open on several sides more, so they can look around and relax!

Also remember that when you place the pet carrier in the car, always remember to use the seat belts! Many models of carriers allow hooking with belts. This is very important because, in the event of an accident, the pet carrier can remain firmly anchored to the seat, keeping your pet safe.

Another useful accessory is the dividing net, ideal for preventing the dog from accessing the front seats of the car. Distract the driver should be avoided in this case. The advantage of the net is that it leaves the dog a lot of space and freedom of movement. Therefore, it is particularly suitable for long journeys or for dogs that do not tolerate the carrier very much.

Finding dog-friendly accommodations and activities

To make a better trip with your dog, we always advise you to get your dog used to the carrier gradually, starting as a puppy.

We also advise you to bring the pet carrier into the house and to leave your pet free to enter and leave it freely so that it can gain the right confidence.

To entice him to enter the cage for transporting dogs in the car, you can use treats, waiting for the time necessary for him to climb into the carrier by himself, perhaps spurring him on with a little push but without forcing his movement. It is essential to link transport to a happy experience, so the first few times it is advisable to take the dog to the park or the sea, avoiding that the memory of the kennel is combined with an unpleasant visit to the vet.

You can try inserting a cover or a toy inside that makes your puppy feel at ease! In short, getting your dog used to the kennel is very important to face the journey without stress and in total serenity for both.

Here are some tips on how to best get our dog used to the seat belt:

✓ Always show it to him, even in moments of relaxation, so that it does not appear to be a totally foreign accessory to him

149

✓ Try to get him to wear it and, when you can, reward him with a tasty snack or some positive reinforcement

✓ When it's time to wear the belt, offer your pet a game or a fun activity, so he can distract himself!

One of the things to do with the dog that you will surely always be able to practice, to make him feel at ease, even when travelling, is giving your dog a massage. Manual touch could be helpful for our dog to get more positive and friendly ways of behaving, developing at the same time empathy. Furthermore, the most comfortable place for the dog to practice this exercise is certainly at home, but it can very well be done while travelling, camping or at the end of a long walk in the mountains.

Finally, it is essential to follow some useful advice, to leave the dog calm when traveling by car and avoid problems:

✓ The animal must not be fed before transport, as it could suffer from car sickness and get nervous.

✓ It is important to make the dog drink enough and keep him hydrated, especially during longer journeys.

✓ It is advisable to make stops at least every two hours, to let the animal walk and offer it the opportunity to do its business.

✓ The dog should never be made to look out the window, to avoid eye problems due to wind and dust.

✓ It is important to drive carefully and not to turn on the air conditioning but leave the windows slightly open to ensure correct air circulation inside the passenger compartment.

With these final tips concludes our complete guide on how to train and keep our dogs happy and healthy. Any topic was addressed, from puppy education to mental health, to hygiene, up to adult dog training. We are sure that now you will have all the tools, advice and knowledge available to ensure that your dog can be well educated, properly trained, clean and in perfect health. All you have to do is start applying these tips and provide the best for your dog.

34442776R00084